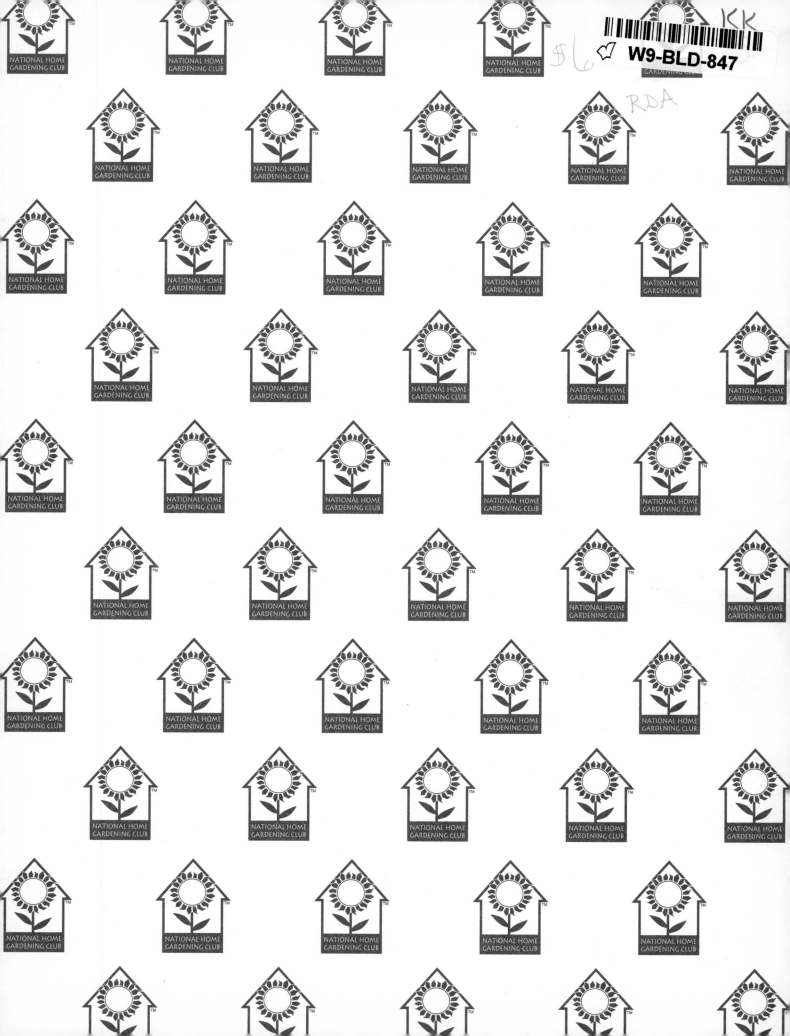

Garden Rewards

*Member Insights &
Ideas*

NATIONAL HOME
GARDENING CLUB

Acknowledgements

Garden Rewards—Member Insights & Ideas

Copyright© 1998 National Home Gardening Club

Mike Vail
Vice President, Product Marketing/Business Development

Tom Carpenter
Director of Book and New Media Development

A. Cort Sinnes
Home Gardener's Library Executive Editor

Kelly March O'Hara
Executive Director, National Home Gardening Club

Dan Kennedy
Book Production Manager

Michele Teigen
Book Development Coordinator

Gina Germ
Photo Editor

Principal photography provided by Dave Brus

Illustrations by K&K Studios

Gina Seeling
Art Direction

A special thanks to photographers Walter Chandoha, Bill Johnson, Jim Block and Amy Sumner, and all the members who also submitted photos and illustrations.

10 9 8 7 6 5 4 3 2 1

ISBN 1-58159-018-0

National Home Gardening Club

12301 Whitewater Drive

Minnetonka, MN 55343

Table of Contents

There's no doubt about it—gardening is fun and rewarding. Why else would National Home Gardening Club members dig in every year to create and maintain some of our country's most beautiful and productive home gardens? Annuals, perennials, vegetables, shrubs, trees...all bring happiness to our lives and rewards to our hearts.

But there's another side to gardening too—the hard work and (sometimes) frustration that goes with growing something worthwhile. There's nothing like tending your sweet corn all summer long only to have your raccoon neighbors harvest your crop the day before it is to ripen to perfection. Or waiting to see a new plant's first blossom, only to have it get torn up in an unwanted wind storm.

Every gardener has stories from both sides of the gardening coin. So, to help you experience more of the joys and rewards, and avoid pitfalls and frustrations, we went straight to one of the best sources we know—NHGC Members!

Because while no one knows everything about gardening, everyone knows something and has some good ideas. When you put a bunch of that knowledge together, you get an invaluable, insight-filled book like *Garden Rewards—Member Insights & Ideas.*

Winnowing down to the actual tips that made this book, from all the submissions we received, wasn't easy. But we did keep an eye out for special ideas and unique strategies that would be invaluable to a wide variety of members—from those with acres of land, to homeowners with a city lot, as well as apartment dwellers with a balcony's worth of containers to work with.

Of course, not every tip will work for every gardener. And any one idea may not work across the country, in the state next door or even across the street. But what we can promise you is this: The strategies, techniques, hints and tips in this book are effective and have proven successful for a fellow NHGC member. The knowledge is sound, and every idea and solution shared here is worth a try.

So whether you live in the North, South, East or West; your garden is in Zone 9 or Zone 2 or somewhere in between; you love annuals, perennials, vegetables, roses, shrubs, houseplants or trees; you garden for or to attract wildlife or both...there's knowledge awaiting you in this book.

Dig in and enjoy!

Justin Hancock
Editor for *Garden Rewards—Members Insights & Ideas*

Container
Success

Container gardening continues to grow in popularity — because the results are beautiful, of course, but also because gardening in containers helps you solve many of the challenges associated with traditional gardening. In fact, sometimes container gardening is a tip in itself, when other growing techniques, cures and remedies fail. Here you'll find members' ideas for interesting containers, plenty of ideas for what to grow in them, and tips for taking care of the plants for beautiful results ... all combining to bring you container success.

Try container gardening . . .

If you plant in big pots and want something lightweight for drainage, put big pine cones in the bottom of the pot. They are good for drainage, decompose and are good for the soil. (Some people say Styrofoam packing peanuts work too, but they're a mess when you dump the pots out in the compost pile; plus you have to be sure they aren't the kind that dissolve in water.)

Mary Brooks Bethune, South Carolina

Herbal houseplants

Rosemary, bay and lemongrass are tender perennials that make good houseplants. If you grow the plants outside, dig them about three weeks before the first predicted frost. Dig them with a generous ball of soil. With a sharp knife, slice away about an inch or two of the rootball. Line a clay flowerpot with gravel and a compost-sand mixture. Insert your herb, fill the space between with more of the compost mixture and water the plant in. Leave it outdoors in the shade for a week and then bring it indoors.

WHGC Staff

container gardening

Container gardening is great

Container gardening is great—there's less bending over and less weeding and fewer animal problems. Plus, you can move the containers as you like. To help make the containers even more attractive, place them on different levels so they are at different heights. It's very attractive.

Mildred Tyler
Lucerne Valley, California

Re-use plastic lids

Instead of purchasing plastic plant trays I use old lids underneath my houseplants. The water still drains out of the containers, and the flexible plastic lids don't get as brittle as expensive store bought trays, so they last longer.

WHGC Staff

Memorable containers

When my children grew up and left home, I wasn't sure what to do with their child-hood toys. My children didn't want to take them, and the toys provided me with such precious memories. I thought I could use the toys as summer planters. Besides being attractive, they also rekindle my summer memories. You can also find many suitable toys at garage sales.

Rose Zak
Brainerd, Minnesota

Instant humidity

Plants need a lot more humidity than the amount in most homes. To get more humidity: Put your African violet, or other houseplant on a tray of small pebbles. Allow the pebbles to be almost covered in water. As the water evaporates, it humidifies the air around your plant. Don't allow the water to touch the bottom of the pot, though.

Judy Patchel
San Diego, California

Transplanting task

I grow about 20 citrus trees in large clay pots. At times, the trees have to be transplanted. This is a major task. I asked several nurseries what the best way to do this is and they offered ill-fated solutions that resulted in damaged roots or broken pots (expensive pots, at that). My wife suggested I put a garden hose to the bottom drainage hole of the pot and turn the hose on full-force, holding it tight to the hole. I tried it and the rootball slid right out of the pot. It has worked for me more than 50 times now.

James Thompson
San Antonio, Texas

Where does the water go?

If you use wine barrels as containers to grow plants in, they should have at least 3 inches of drain holes at the bottom, either three 1-inch holes, 4-inch holes, or 6-inch holes. When you use saucers for drainage, elevate the pot inside slightly so water can freely flow out of the holes (instead of being blocked by the flat surface of the saucer).

Phillip Greig
Walnut Creek, California

Color check

If you have containers in full sun, look for lighter-colored ones. Dark containers can absorb a lot of heat, and too much heat can hurt plants' roots.

WHGC Staff

Winter color with little work

Colorado has a very short gardening season, so here is my little trick for bringing some springtime indoors for our long, snowy winter. I plant my geraniums in 22-inch faux-terracotta pots that sit on trays with rollers under them. The geraniums enjoy the short summer on the deck of my log home, and they spend winters in my sunny west windows, continuing to bloom their little hearts out. (I also save on dirt and my back by filling my huge pots halfway with empty soda cans and putting dirt over them. Recycling at its best!)

Debi Renn
Fort Collins,
Colorado

Look for the tall ones

Look for taller containers instead of lower, wider ones. The taller containers have better drainage (if they have holes at the bottom). Better drainage means less chance of root rot.

WHGC Staff

Control the water

Flower power

If you want to encourage blooming in your African violet, add a capful of hydrogen peroxide to a quart of water and then water as usual.

Amos Graber
Montgomery, Indiana

Neat houseplants!

You can get cheap and fun houseplants by planting the seeds of avocado, citrus fruits and mango—as well as many other fruits that you get from the grocery store—instead of just throwing them away. Most are easy to start and make interesting plants. (They might not ever produce fruit, though, in indoor conditions.)

Cheryl Porche
Abita Springs, Louisiana

flow

Water-saving tip

To keep from wasting water while watering my outside baskets, I fill up an inexpensive cooler with water and then soak my baskets.

Rick & Kathy Dixon
Temple, Texas

Great Designs

We gardeners spend so much time thinking about how to make our plants thrive, sometimes we forget what can be one of the simplest pleasures and most enjoyable aspects of our pastime—designing the garden in the first place. Simply put, a great garden has the right plants in the right places. So here are member ideas and tips (tried-and-true and all-new) for placing those plants so they work together ... in one attractive, great design.

The right plants in the right places...

Here's a perennial combination that works really well. Try 'Stella D'Oro' daylilies with 'Butterfly Blue' scabiosa. You'll have a great color combination and continuous bloom through the season.

Kathryn D'Alessandro
Greenville, Pennsylvania

Good Screening

Tall annuals and perennials are good for screening areas in the summer. Some, such as sunflowers, bugbanes and macleaya, grow more than 6 feet tall and are great for separating different areas of the garden to give them their own identity.

WHGC Staff

Seasonal pizzazz

Designer gardens

You can make your own garden design by placing tracing paper overlays on a photograph or plot plan. That way, you know what the design will look like. It's lots of fun and helps to cure the winter doldrums.

Patricia Hicks
Portland, Oregon

Sometimes nice indoor plants also make good bedding plants. I use wandering Jew in front of my house—the wonderful purple color of the leaves catches the eye of every passerby. It makes a pleasing sight and they are easy to care for. In autumn, I can take cuttings and have them in the house during winter.

Cammay Baloun
Sioux Falls, South Dakota

Water pizzazz

You can float a gazing ball in water to create a special effect in the water garden. Use aquarium sealer around the nipple and cork of the ball. You can tie it under water to anchor it or let it float freely. Remove the ball in freezing weather.

Carol Turley
Cadiz, Kentucky

I keep my names of hybrid iris and daylilies in an old address book. They are in alphabetical order for easy reference. The small book is easy to carry in my purse or pocket so that I can have my list with me all the time.

*Theresa McDaniel
Holcomb,
Mississippi*

Sneaky flower beds

If you have an area with really poor soil, put down bags of potting soil. Make a small slit in the top of the bag (with drainage holes poked in the bottom of the bag) and plant summer annuals and mulch over the bag. The bags can be left in place until next spring when you can plant in them again. They look great.

*Eloise Barker
Conway, South Carolina*

The little things

Keep a gardening journal. It helps you to see patterns in your garden during a season, and it really helps if you keep the journal year after year and refer to it.

Deborah Reis
Alpharetta, Georgia

If you divide your gardens up in beds (especially raised beds), don't make them too wide so you can't reach the middle from either side. This makes them easier to care for.

WHGC Staff

that count

For an eye-catching way to display vines, such as clematis, plant a vine near an evergreen. The vine will climb up the evergreen and look nice while its roots are shaded by the evergreen. (Be careful not to plant a vine that is too vigorous and will cover up the evergreen, though.)

N. Gaylor
Little Rock, Arkansas

Plant pals

Plant pals

When you plant peppers or other fruiting plants, plant two in a hole. Doing this helps in pollination so you get more fruits. The plants can also help support each other. You save space in the garden, too.

*Rod Jenison
Somerville,
New Jersey*

Pretty tasty treats

Plant your herbs, fruits and vegetables (such as tomatoes and peppers) amongst your ornamentals; most are pretty in their own right. I edge beds with strawberries and fill in bare spots with chives, parsley, basil and oregano. You do need to be careful about what chemicals you might use in the garden.

*Laura Fish
Schaumburg,
Illinois*

Make a nursery

I have a small yard to do my gardening in. To keep as much bloom in the front garden as possible, I start my biennials from seed and transplant the seedlings to spots in the backyard for their first year. The next spring, I move the plants to the front beds where I want color. This staging helps keep the front garden colorful all season. I also stage my slow-growing perennials in the back and move them to the front when they're blooming age. Sometimes I even let plants bloom in the back so I know what color they are and place them accordingly in the front.

*Ernest McKenzie
Prineville, Oregon*

Get more

Changing light

Be really careful when you go selecting your site in early spring. Areas of sun and part shade will change drastically not only because the trees leaf out, but also because the sun's angle will change in midsummer and be completely different.

Freddy Bishop
Gadsden, Alabama

No wasted space

If you have beds of spring bulbs, there's a space in your garden once they're done blooming. I use this area for container gardening for growing my vegetables. It's like having two gardens.

Sharyl Olson
Bertha, Minnesota

Enjoy your garden in or out

Look out of one of your windows in the house next time you want to make a new flower bed. Think of a private garden that you can view just outside of your window instead of having to enjoy it only from someplace outside.

B. Schneider
Pine Bush, New York

from your garden

For an interesting flower bed, try finding an old boat or canoe. If you fill it with strawberries or flowers, it will look delightful in the yard. I have a cement boy sitting in my boat.

Gerri Aylor
Praque, Oklahoma

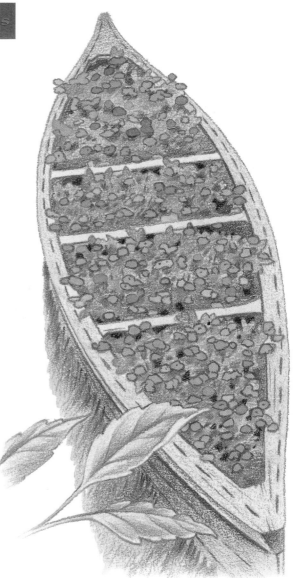

Special places

When planting yummy chocolate mint, separate it from all of your other plants. Like other mints, it will spread really fast and become invasive in the garden. (Planting it in containers is a good idea.)

Theresa Dittmar
Dubuque, Iowa

Mix 'em and

Any garden can be turned into a fruit orchard with containers and planting in odd little spaces. I grow figs in containers, blueberries in with my ornamentals and strawberries tucked here and there.

*Deborah Reis
Alpharetta, Georgia*

Repeat annual

Allow your plants to work for you. Learn your leaves and plant self-sowing annuals in your garden. They'll save you time and money because they come back. If you know what the leaves look like, you can weed without worrying about what you're pulling out.

*Gail Skrip
Oxford,
Massachusetts*

Garden on the rocks

To really make a landscaping job look nice when using field stones, try to place them so they look very natural, even if you have to dig a hole to "plant" them.

*Bruce Gilbert
Valparaiso, Indiana*

match 'em

When planting climbing roses, also plant a clematis. It will wind its way through the rose bush and will be in bloom when the roses aren't. Sometimes they both bloom together. It's a great way to get loads of color in the garden.

Carolyn Moore
Robinson, Illinois

Protecting catnip

I grow catnip with a 3-foot piece of small square wire fence around it. My cats eat the small shoots that I allow to grow through the fence, but the main crop stays safe.

Jan Richter
Fruita, Colorado

Your calendar

Keeping track of the garden

I use an oversized coil-bound calendar with plenty of room under each date to record, on a daily basis, all of the gardening information I'll need to make decisions next year. I record the dates I sowed seeds, how well they germinated and when I planted, potted and set them out. I also note the amount of rainfall, any extreme weather and the types of pest control I've used. This gives me both a "garden" to reflect on during the colder months and a workbook for making decisions about the garden next year.

Marilyn Chaon
West Brooklyn,
Illinois

Conserve water

I live in the middle of a dry desert in Arizona. We plant our melons around the base of our fruit trees, where they shade the trees' roots and share the water. We get both beautiful fruit and melons, and as we haul our water out into the garden, this makes every drop count and lets us expand our garden without extra work.

Shirley Williams
Golden Valley, Arizona

Stake down

I stake down sheets of landscaping fabric between the rows of my garden. The landscaping fabric makes weeding unnecessary and makes the rows look neat and less muddy. If you want to cover the entire garden with the fabric, all you have to do is cut X-shaped holes through the fabric to plant your plants.

Kathleen Quinn
Antioch, Illinois

Warm invitation

Here's a design trick that works for me: Bright colored flowers, especially red ones, can be placed by the front door of your home to draw attention there and make for a cheerful welcome.

Lee & Janey Gust
Brandon, South Dakota

Remember plants

Here's how I keep track of what I've planted and the growing instructions. I cut out the paragraph blurb from last year's catalog for each seed type, and then paste that on a blank sheet of paper. All of the carrots go on one sheet, all of the tomatoes on another, and so on. This way, I have all of the information I need at a glance and I can carry the sheets to the potting shed or even the garden.

Toni Heisey
San Diego, California

the snow

If you want a head start on your garden design, wait until after a light snow and walk in your yard, making footprints where you want the beds to be. Sprinkle a line of wood ashes over your footprints. In spring, your lines will be there already. If you wait until spring to design, you can use a garden hose laid out in the desired shape of your beds.

Walter Chandoha
Annandale, New Jersey

Stop those weeds!

Have trouble with weeds in the rows in your garden? Put your excess grass clippings down in between the rows or on pathways. The grass clippings keep the weeds down, keep you less muddy and are organic when they break down, so they're good for everything.

Donna Fay Hilliard
Odessa, Texas

Garden Potpourri

Members submitted hundreds of great tips for this book, but some of those ideas just don't fall cleanly into one category or the other. And that is to be expected, when an activity as diverse and multifaceted as gardening is the subject. So here's a collection of those miscellaneous bits of lore, from how to keep your hands cleaner in the garden to getting the most out of your clematis. You're sure to find nuggets of valuable knowledge here ... in this special collection of garden potpourri.

What a collective bit of lore ...

Pretty and useful!

Plant sunflower seeds and pumpkins around the bottom of your bird feeder for summer and fall color and to help hide the weed seeds that germinate from the feeder.

Laura Carviou
Marinette, Wisconsin

Pinching mums

When your mums get about 8 inches tall (or at the end of June) pinch back the stems 2 to 3 inches. The mums will fill out tremendously and may begin blossoming earlier.

Dawn Crook
Wyoming, Michigan

Planting feed

I wanted to grow sunflowers to attract birds to my garden. Instead of buying many expensive packets of seeds, I bought a 10-pound bag of sunflower bird feed. I planted the "feed" and got great results at a cheaper price.

Lorraine Trevino
Floresville, Texas

Gardeners of tomorrow

To help children get an early interest in gardening, I encourage them while they're young. One good way to do this is by letting them plant seeds (particularly large seeds, such as peas, beans, sunflowers and nasturtiums are best) in clear plastic glasses. The kids can watch the roots develop, and after the roots show through the glass, they'll know it's time to transplant. They can then have the plants in their gardens.

Mr. & Mrs. David Merchant
North San Juan, California

Escape route

To help prevent accidental drownings of birds and small animals in a water garden, always give them a means of escape if they fall in. A well-seasoned piece of driftwood can be placed from the edge of the pool and extend into it. You can also provide a ladder of rocks. Visitors appreciate a safe approach to get a drink of water or bath.

Carol Turley
Cadiz, Kentucky

The straight and narrow

Straight rows are easy to work with in the garden. If you have trouble making rows straight, space your long-handled garden tools parallel to each other with enough of a space in between for you to work. Press down the handles of the tools to make your straight rows.

Walter Chandoha
Annandale, New Jersey

It is worth the time

To increase the spread between two rose canes you wish to keep but are too close together, cut a length from a pruned branch and secure this piece on a thorn on each cane. It may take several tries to find the right length, but it's worth the effort.

Leslie Sands
Los Osos, California

Party favorites

You can make great place cards for parties by growing an herb in a nice lithographed tomato sauce can with the guest's name written on a plant label. Be careful not to over water as you'll have no drainage holes. Fill a third of the can with fine gravel or pebbles, and add a thin layer of soil mix. Insert the seedling, add more mix and gently firm it around the plant. Your guests can keep the herb containers as mementos of your party.

WHGC Staff

Garden ideas that

Housing for friendly toads

When I have a clay flowerpot that has a small piece of the side broke off, instead of throwing it out, I turn it upside down and place it in the garden. It makes a little toad house, and toads eat many insects in the garden. This way I can recycle and encourage garden friends at the same time.

Mae Byers
White Sulphur Springs,
West Virginia

Cleaning crystal

Living in Fresno, I have always had a problem with mineral deposits on just about anything my water touched. Therefore, I have always been hesitant to use my good lead crystal vases, not wanting to get ugly water marks on them. I discovered that a few drops of household bleach added to the water in the vase prevents the water marks.

Mary Sheridan
Fresno, California

A quick way to whip something up

I keep a case of canning jars and a roll of gingham ribbon with my gardening supplies. That way I can quickly step into the garden and put together a vase of flowers, complete with a bow, as a host or hostess gift for those impromptu summer barbecues.

Christine Green
Imperial, Missouri

Make your own rose!

If you have room for more roses, try pollinating the ones you have with a watercolor brush. To pollinate a rose, take a fine paintbrush and rub off some yellow, powdery pollen onto it. Then transfer this pollen to the sticky part of the center of another rose. Once the flower fades, a hip will form with the seeds inside. Then, when the rose hips are ripe, plant individual seeds in a flat with sandy loam. You may find you have a variety of bushes different from the source ones. It's fun to see the baby plants develop. Don't forget to water!

Doris Roach
Bellflower, California

Great gifts

Whenever I purchase a packet of seeds, I plant some in my garden and some in a pot for a special person, who then receives the plant. Teenagers in particular, love this.

Avis Amann
Kingman, Arizona

Plants are great

Pruning flowering shrubs

If your flowering shrubs bloom before the strawberries are ripe, prune them right away after blooming. (Examples are lilac, forsythia, mock orange and some azalea.) Those shrubs that flower after the strawberry season are best pruned in early spring. If you need to do heavy pruning, stagger the pruning over a couple of years so you still get bloom.

WHGC Staff

Recycling newspaper

When you're setting out trees or shrubs, put shredded newspaper at the bottom of the hole, then put the plant on top. (The newspaper adds organic matter and some small amounts of nutrients.)

Mary Dingler
Cedartown, Georgia

Getting under the skin

At harvest and canning season, here's a tip for skinning a tomato. Hold a ripe tomato in one hand and stroke it with the back (dull side) of a paring knife. Rub the knife all over the tomato. Now cut the core out of the tomato and the skin will slip right off. (This sure beats the hot water method!)

Rose Mary Fletcher
Decatur, Illinois

Working smart

Two gifts in one

I like to use clay flowerpots instead of gift bags or boxes to package the gifts for my gardening friends. You can wrap them in cellophane like an Easter basket. It's very appropriate!

Kristi Speed
Vacaville,
California

Don't waste that water

I recycle from my pond: Instead of wasting the water from my pond when I clean it out, I use it to water my flowers, especially the potted ones. They really love it.

Rowena Farley
Carthage, Missouri

It's good to dead-head (but not to be one!)

Dead-heading might be a pain-in-the-neck, but it is essential to maintaining a beautiful cutting garden. It's also good for keeping your perennials healthy and encouraging more blooms. (The energy of the plant goes back to the plant instead of going to the seeds.)

Randolph Fitz-Hugh
New Orleans, Louisiana

Morning chore

I only water my plants in the morning before 8 a.m. Watering then saves water (less is lost due to evaporation), and it reduces fungal diseases caused by water sitting on the leaves at night.

Katherine McCartney
Olympia, Washington

Keep your hands clean

To make washing your hands easier after working the soil, apply a light covering of Vaseline or hand lotion to your hands before starting your chore.

Wanda Bonno
Denver, Colorado

Get kids interested

I had to constantly tell neighbor children to stay out of our yard until I showed them the plants and invited them to help me in the garden. Because of their involvement, they stay out of my flowers now.

Nancy Martin
Lancaster, New York

Jamming in the garden

I like to carry a small cassette player along with me in the garden. I carry it in my gardening apron and listen to audio tapes. Long garden jobs seems to go much faster when you're listening to a good book. Plus, it's free from the public library!

Alixe Andrews
Pine City, New York

Gourd drying

To dry gourds, I hang them up somewhere after the stem has dried. It's important to let the air flow all around the gourd. Let it dry until you hear the seeds rattle inside. After that, scrub any mold off the gourds with a scouring pad. They're ready to be painted or made into a bird house.

Shirley Lewis
Lancaster,
Kentucky

File system

I like to cut the articles out of gardening magazines that are useful. I file the articles in folders by subject. It is so much easier to locate them when I need them.

Sue Cerny
Saint Johns,
Michigan

A great way to relax

Relax in the garden

I work full-time and often come home from work still full of the day's stress. I get home and I know all that I have to do in the evening (cooking, dishes, laundry, cleaning, that sort of thing). Sometimes it adds to the stress. All summer, when I get home every day, I stick my little hand pruners in my pocket and go and walk around the yard. While I'm admiring how well all my plants are doing, I snip off the dead blossoms and pull weeds as I see them. By the time I'm done, my stress is pretty much gone, the flower beds look good, and I'm ready to continue my day. I get my work done by doing just a little bit everyday instead of having one big job to do at once.

Carol Davis
Racine, Wisconsin

Overwinter a geranium

We overwinter our geraniums. All you need to do is dry the geranium before the season is over, but before frost. Store the plant bare-root in a brown paper bag in a cool, dry place over winter. In March, pot the plants, and cut them down to 6 to 8 inches tall. Start watering them and place them in the light. The plant will grow new leaves and be ready to plant outside in late May.

Robert Scannell
Kewaskum,
Wisconsin

Don't let them escape!

To put in spreading perennials that are invasive in a small spot in the garden, and keep them there, use a Styrofoam cooler. Just cut off the bottom of the cooler, and sink it down into the soil. If you plant inside the cooler, the roots of the plant are confined in the cooler and the plant won't escape into the garden.

Bob Keyser
Swanton, Ohio

Fresh basil in winter

Cut fresh basil, wash it then dry it. Rub both sides of the leaves with olive oil and then put in the freezer. You can use them as you would fresh.

*Fran Malone
Cincinnati, Ohio*

Don't cry!

While cutting your onions, try lighting a votive candle to avoid the burning of the eyes and crying.

*Rollin Phillips
Rochester, New York*

Keep it contained

If you like a plant but know it's invasive, get a large plastic bucket from your deli and use it to contain your plant. All you need to do is cut out the bottom of the bucket and sink the bucket into the ground. Then plant your plant inside the bucket so it can't get out and spread all over your garden.

Gerald Pollock
Hawk Run, Pennsylvania

Beautiful insulation

In the summer, a porch, or even the side of your house can become really hot. This can really heat up the house. I've planted beans to climb up some lattice I put up to shade the side of the porch and make it cooler.

Jan Sadauskas
Arlington,
Washington

Remember your friends

Be careful about using any chemicals to kill insects in the butterfly garden. The chemicals might kill the caterpillars that will turn into the butterflies you're trying to attract.

Marian McNabb
Linn Grove, Iowa

Anyone can have cotton

Gardeners in the North, or where they have short summers, can grow cotton for fun. All you have to do is harvest the cotton pods before winter comes and then put the pods into the microwave for a couple of minutes to open up the pods and harvest the fluffy cotton.

Anitha Berthcsi
Philadelphia,
Pennsylvania

A garden mystery solved

Do you have really alkaline soil? Is it tough to get the pH down? If so, consider testing your tap water—mine was 8.2. (In many areas, water has carbonates that really raise the pH.)

James Grealy
Glenview, Illinois

Propagate willows

To grow pussy willows, stick a cut cane in the ground about 6 inches deep at the edge of a body of water. The plants seem to really do well in wet areas. They are easy to grow and propagate if they're kept moist enough.

Roni Spitler Davis
Appleton City, Missouri

Keep the floor clean

I keep some old plastic bags near my backdoor whenever I'm working in the yard or garden. If I have to run into the house for just a minute a two, I can slip the bags on over my dirty or muddy shoes. That way my floors stay cleaner.

Rhonda Watson
Reedley, California

Helping the birds

To clean your bird bath, put a small amount of bleach in with a little water. Then use a cleaner such as Soft-Scrub brand and rinse well. This will help to kill germs and diseases that could hurt the birds.

Judy Rank
Sylvania, Ohio

Personalized melon baskets

I've found something fun to serve at a brunch or dinner that makes quite a conversation piece. Make a melon basket with your name carved in the handle. Take a melon and cut your design using a small sharp knife. Scoop out the melon with a melonballer. Put the melon scoops in a separate container. Clean out the entire melon, but be careful not to remove too much of the rind. You can carve your name or a message on the edge or on a handle. Wash some fruit to add to the basket and add some fresh mint sprigs. Serve chilled.

Karlin DiMarcello
Powell, Tennessee

Buckle up your buds

Flower carrier

If you need to drive with cut flowers in the car but are worried about spilling, here's a solution. Slip a cardboard box into a plastic bag with handles (handles make it easier to carry). Put a one pound can in each corner of the box and a quart size jar or rose vase in the middle with your flowers. You can arrive at your destination with no water spilled.

Mrs. Bowden
Tulsa, Oklahoma

Permanent backdrops

For gardeners with limited time or energy, a backdrop of evergreens provides privacy, a pretty view and easy maintenance. The trees look great as they grow and cost less than a privacy fence. Many birds also like to nest and rest in the trees. If you have a little more time or energy, you can plant flowers or other types of greenery in front of the trees.

Gayle McIntosh
Clifton Forge,
Virginia

Gardening is

Don't believe all you hear

Check with your local state university cooperative extension agency with questions before believing all you read. Sometimes books and magazines get things mixed up. (The agencies have agents trained to answer your toughest questions.)

Joan Chiang
Littleton, Colorado

Clematis hint

Clematis can be really finicky. One thing you can do to help keep your plants healthy is to keep the roots of your vines shaded. It makes them thrive.

Mrs. Webster Whitney
Nashua,
New Hampshire

Hand therapy while gardening

I have a tip to help prevent dried out hands and shredded cuticles that come along with gardening in the soil. Get some cuticle cream, hand moisturizer, cotton moisture gloves and mud gloves (the gloves that have been dipped in rubber). Apply cuticle cream to the cuticles but don't rub it completely in. Then apply an ample amount of hand moisturizer to the hands. Place your cotton moisture gloves on, then the mud gloves. Your hands will receive a nice treatment while you work away! (Plus, your hands won't smell like dirty gardening gloves.)

Rhonda Foley
Snowmass Village, Colorado

good for your hands

Garden ornament for the birds

To help encourage kids to watch birds, have them make a bird feeder. One easy way is to smear a large pine cone in peanut butter and hang it up outside where the kids can see the birds that come to it.

Courtney Wilson
Summerville, South Carolina

Even onion skins can be recycled

Don't throw out any yellow onion skins. At Easter, you can make tie-dyed eggs in shades of white and yellow. Here's how: Put the onion skins in a large bowl of cold water. Cut 8- to 9-inch squares of cheesecloth, according to how many eggs you would like to dye. Using raw eggs, cover each egg with wet onion skins. Lay the egg on a square of cheesecloth and tie two of the opposite corners together. This holds the onion skins next to the egg. When the eggs are wrapped, put them in cold water, bring to a boil, then lower heat to a slow simmer for about 20 minutes. When the eggs are done, drain the hot water and fill the pan with cold running water. Carefully cut the cheesecloth off the eggs and enjoy the lovely one-of-a-kind eggs you've made. You can also fill mesh bags with onion skins and lay them down near plants you usually have pest problems with. This worked very well for me last summer.

Mary Louise Chulak
Beaver Falls, Pennsylvania

Let it snow.

Take advantage of snow

I live in a cold, high mountain area. The winters are quite harsh. To protect my roses and other ornamental perennials, I heap snow on them. Snow helps protect plants from the drying winds and helps keep the soil temperature more even. In spring, I don't have to pile it off like you do mulch.

Dawn Holmes
Indian Valley, Idaho

Winter joy/summer blooms

In the fall, I save one or two of my potted impatiens and put them into a sunny window indoors to winter over. In March, I take slips off the plants and remove the blossoms and lower leaves of the slips. I pot them directly into light potting soil in the small containers (packs) that I bought them and my vegetables in last spring. I dip each slip in water and dust it lightly with rooting hormone before putting the slip in a hole made with a pencil in the soil. I usually do about three slips a day so I have enough plants for my beds and baskets. I don't need to buy impatiens again.

Harriet Link
Renville, Minnesota

...let it snow

Hard-boiled water

When I boil eggs, I let the water cool, then use it to water my flowering plants with instead of wasting it. I put the shells in my compost pile, too.

Lance Howard
Des Moines, Iowa

Rose covers

To make cheap rose covers for winter: Cut several long branches and stick them in the ground around a rose bush. Stuff the area with hay and tie the top into a teepee. You can weave softer branches before stuffing the hay in to make a basket-like covering.

Patricia Ihloff
Plainfield, Connecticut

Beating
Pests

Most gardeners would agree:
When asked to name gardening's
biggest challenge, the answer
always seems to focus on pests and
how to defeat them before they ruin
your beautifully growing garden
and cancel out all your hard work.
Pests are real, whether it's deer
clipping off the first signs of color
in spring, or aphids sucking the life
from your roses. No matter what
the challenge, these tips and solutions have worked for another
member, somewhere, before.
Give one a try... and enjoy beating
those pests.

Members offer solutions to the challenge…

Stop scale in your garden

To prevent problems with scale or borers on your fruit trees, try tying an old nylon stocking with a bar of Octagon brand soap inside to a low branch.

Tami Wells
Baton Rouge, Louisiana

Re-use citrus peels

Kitty protection

I had problems with cats using my garden as their litterbox. What I do now is spread my citrus peels around my plants. The cats stay away.

Helen Holth
Carrington, North Dakota

Anti-deer mix

There's a spray I use to keep deer out of my garden. I mix one tablespoon garlic powder with two ounces of hot sauce and one pint of water. I mix it in the blender and pour it in a gallon sprayer filled with water. You need to spray after each rain, though.

Rudolph Bensen
Bruceton,
Tennessee

Bulb insurance

If you have problems with animals trying to eat your bulbs, try planting them in the baskets you get fruits in from the grocery store. The animals won't be able to get through the plastic mesh and eat your bulb. (It won't keep them away from the blossoms, though.)

Amy Sneeden
Lake Norden,
South Dakota

Save your houseplants from bugs outside

When putting out houseplants for spring, sprinkle some garlic powder in the pot. Do this once a month afterwards to help keep insects off of the plants and out of the soil.

Hazel Burney
Wichita Falls, Texas

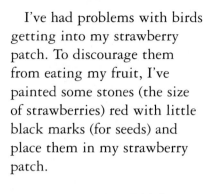

Keep your strawberries safe

I've had problems with birds getting into my strawberry patch. To discourage them from eating my fruit, I've painted some stones (the size of strawberries) red with little black marks (for seeds) and place them in my strawberry patch.

Mary Jane Flikke
San Antonio, Texas

Painting the str

Squirrels on birdfeeders

If you have a problem with squirrels in the garden, put up a bird or squirrel feeder to feed them. If they have their own feeder, they won't need to eat things in your garden or ransack your yard.

George Willard
Blasdell, New York

A fence for deer

I used to have a big problem with deer. I use heavy string or twine to make a fence out of ,to keep the deer out of the garden and flower bed. It works for me and it's a lot cheaper than buying fence.

Mary Noel
Hamilton, New York

Homemade bug repellent

I use a mixture of Dove brand dishwashing soap, Listerine and water to fight off bugs on my flowers and shrubs during the summer. (Mix about a tablespoon of soap and a tablespoon of Listerine to a gallon of water and then spray your plants thoroughly once a week.)

*L. Benton-King
Duluth, Georgia*

A homemade fence

I own a large dog that likes to disturb my flower beds. That's why I built a good-looking fence to keep him out. The fence is made of $1/2$-inch PVC plastic pipe and $1/2$-inch 90-degree elbows and $1/2$-inch t-fittings. It works great!

*Terry Bennett
Sioux City, Iowa*

If you notice hornworms on your tomatoes, but the worms have white spots on them, don't kill them. The spots are from a parasitic wasp that kills the hornworms. Keeping those worms alive will give you more wasps (parasitic wasps aren't the ones that bother picnics across the country).

Walter Chandoha
Annandale,
New Jersey

The good

A hint for fire ants

I've had a great deal of trouble with fire ants. In the past I've controlled them with chemical sprays, which worked, but they made me uncomfortable because I have grandchildren and a dog. So when I found a fire ant mound in the middle of my flower bed, I decided to sprinkle the mound heavily with baking soda, and much to my surprise, it worked immediately. They abandoned their mound soon afterwards. It might be worth a try for other members.

Joanne Schmidt
Colbert, Georgia

Pest control recipe

Ground cayenne peppers and place the powder in some unscented laundry soap in water. Use this for pest control in the landscape.

David Harrell
Talbott, Tennessee

Cayenne

bad and ugly

Slug protection

To control slugs in your garden, try surrounding your planting area with corrugated aluminum lawn edging. Simply install the edging as usual, but then use a pliers to bend the top part of the edging into a 1-inch lip that faces out. You'll find that slugs aren't able to crawl over the lip and the physical barrier will protect tender plants.

Barbara Price
Fairfield, Pennsylvania

Reduce mosquito numbers

Cover yellow plastic lids from coffee cans and containers with the sticky mix Tanglefoot. When you hang them up, mosquitoes become trapped.

Mildred Pudell
Benton Harbor, Michigan

How to scare off deer

To keep deer from eating all of my favorite small trees and to keep rabbits from eating my plants and strawberries, I tie plastic grocery bags to the trees and in the patch. It works really well for me.

Erla Werner
Flasher,
North Dakota

Protect from pocket gophers

If you want to make raised beds but are afraid of pocket gophers tunneling up through them, here's a trick. Lay heavy gauge hardware cloth with holes no larger than a half inch on the bottom of the bed before you fill it with soil. This will prevent the gophers from digging up the plants you have.

Julie Guth
Deerwood,
Minnesota

No more poc

A clean way to keep deer out

I cut slivers of Irish Spring brand soap and tie them to posts in my garden. The soap really helps to keep deer out of the garden. (Pieces of old nylon stockings work well to hold the soap because they allow the scent of the soap to move through the holes.)

Jacquelyn Mousch
Oakland, Maryland

Beneficial bugs

I greenhouse garden and sometimes have problems with aphids. When I do, I use ladybugs to eat the aphids, both inside and out. I also mulch with worm casings, which build the soil and fertilize organically.

Debra Pousson
Baton Rouge, Louisiana

Rabbit-proofing the garden

I don't use chemicals to keep rabbits out of my lettuce patch. Instead, I put plastic windmills around. They spin in the breeze and the rabbits stay away.

C. McLellan
Spencer, Iowa

ket gophers

Keep cats from your houseplants

I have a cat that likes to dig in my potted plants. I've found an easy way to deter him. Cut a slit in a paper plate with a hole at the center and I slip it around the stem of the plant. The plate covers the soil so the cat can't get in. You can also use construction paper.

Lynne McLane
Shelby, Alabama

Raccoons and sweet corn

I have an idea to share about keeping raccoons out of my sweet corn. Try dusting the lowest leaf of several stalks of corn at the ends of the rows and down the outer edges of the patch with red pepper. This has to be repeated after each rain, but it helps.

Shirley Robertson
Versailles, Missouri

Control ants

To control ants in the garden without chemicals, try sprinkling instant grits (uncooked) around the ant beds. The ants eat the grits, the grits expand in their stomachs and presto! No more ants.

Debra Miller
Huntsville, Alabama

Keep raccoons and weeds out

I used to have problems with raccoons, but now I lay sheets of black plastic down outside of my corn and grapes. It keeps raccoons away because they don't like the feel of walking on the plastic.

Norman Crimi
Goshen, Indiana

wanted

Save your hummingbird feeders

I like to set up hummingbird feeders, but I don't like it when ants invade the feeder. I've come up a solution. All you need to do is spray the chain that the feeder hangs on with spray-on hand/body lotion. The treatment lasts for several weeks, and the ants won't climb over the chain.

Cris Samuel
Lexington, South Carolina

A pretty way to stop voles

To deter voles in the garden, plant some fritillarias. The bulbs release an odor in the soil that the voles dislike.

Michele Fergus
Greensboro,
North Carolina

Getting stuck

If you have a problem with whiteflies or fungus gnats on your houseplants, look for yellow sticky cards from your garden center. These cards are bright yellow and covered with an adhesive. The insects are attracted to the cards, and then get stuck on them.

W&GC Staff

Stop pests with mouthwash

An effective spray for garden pests is to mix a little bit of Listerine brand mouthwash in water. Insects stay away—it works every time for me.

Lora Krugman
Phoenix, Arizona

Insects stay

Old-fashioned cat protection

I plant marigolds around my newly planted flower-beds. The cats don't like the smell of marigolds and won't use the beds as a litterbox. That way, I don't have to use any expensive chemicals to keep them out.

Victoria Gutierrez
Temple City,
California

Look here first

Leave a couple of weeds (such as pig-weed) in your garden. Just be careful not to let them go to seed. Many insects will attack the weeds first. When you see insects munching on the weeds, pull the weeds out and treat your garden accordingly.

WHGC Staff

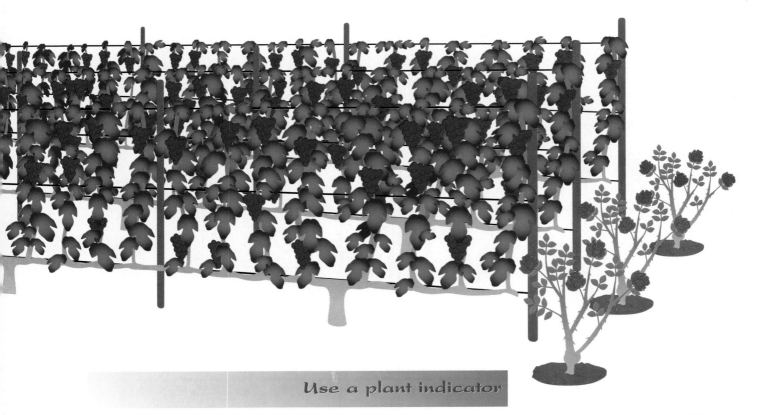

Use a plant indicator

Plant a rosebush at the end of your rows of grapevines if you have a lot of grapes. Pest problems will show on the roses before the grapes. You can deal with the pest sooner, then.

Susan Ertmer
Apple River, Illinois

Keeping birds out

I deter birds from the fruit trees in my garden by stringing amounts of Christmas tree tinsel in my fruit trees. They don't like all the reflected light and leave my trees alone.

Mychele Hutchinson
Crestview, Florida

You can use bird netting to keep pests such as deer and rabbits from munching on your plants.

WHGC Staff

binations

Scary plant combination

Here's a plant combination to scare off aphids. I've found that planting chives or green onions next to my roses keeps the aphids off of my roses.

Everett Morton
Riverside, California

CHIVES

To keep your slugs from eating your hostas and other shade-loving plants, lay a ring of bare copper wire around the plants. Keep the wire free of debris and dirt. Slugs won't cross over the wire. It has worked for me for the past two years.

C.L. Ayers
Reynolds, Georgia

Stop squirrels

When planting bulbs that squirrels favor, complete the planting according to the kind of bulb. When you have covered the bulb to an inch of the top of the hole, add a teaspoon of garlic powder, then fill the hole the rest of the way. I've been told chili powder works, too, but I use garlic.

Bethene Smith
Gahanna, Ohio

Deer-proof your garden

I know someone who has a good trick to keep deer out of the yard. Erect a pole about 8 feet tall in the middle of the garden. Place a motion detector on top with two outlets. In one, put a floodlight bulb and in the other, screw in an outdoor plug-in. Hook a doorbell buzzer up to this. Set the sensitivity level to low so branches waving in the wind won't set it off. The combination of the light and the buzzer discourages the deer (but keep the buzzer on a low enough volume as not to annoy any neighbors).

Walt Lindley
Mount Pleasant, Michigan

To protect my young plants that have been just put outside from cats and other animals, I put plastic forks around them. The animals won't lay down over the forks. It really works for me.

Marlyn Beck
Claysville,
Pennsylvania

Try salt on slugs

Protect your plants from slugs

To kill slugs, I sprinkle a little bit of salt on them. The salt makes them shrivel right up. Be careful of the ground around your plants, though, because the salt can cause damage if there is too much of it.

Kathy Richard
East Lansing, Michigan

Slugs don't like a day at the beach

To deter slugs from destroying my hostas, I sprinkle construction-grade sand over the top of the soil. The slugs don't like to crawl across the sand, and it doesn't look bad. Plus, it's safe for kids and pets. (Don't use this if you have heavy clay soil, though, because the sand can mix with the clay and form a layer impervious to water and plant roots.)

*Thomas Herrmann
Buffalo Grove,
Illinois*

Keep rabbits out

I go to the local barber and use the hair clippings to deter rabbits. The clippings are free and biodegradable in the garden.

*Renee Gazarkiewicz
LaPorte, Indiana*

Double fencing to keep deer out

To keep deer out of the garden, place two fences a couple of feet apart from each other on the edge of the garden. The deer see the second fence behind the first and won't try to jump over it.

Betty Pursglove
Applegate, Oregon

An underground fence

To deter moles and some other kinds of ground-dwelling creatures, bury fine hardware cloth about 6 inches down in your beds. The burrowing animals won't be able to get through the barrier.

WHGC Staff

Starting
Seeds

Starting plants from seed can be tough. Really tough. Fortunately, almost all gardeners need to do it at one time or another, so there are plenty of fellow members' insights and tips to help you achieve success. We present those ideas (some complicated, others easy) for getting your seedlings off to a good start, right here. There's nothing like having a couple dozen gardeners backing you up with their knowledge... and helping you start your seeds successfully.

Sharpen your green thumb . . .

Save those 35 millimeter film canisters you get with film for the camera. If the plastic caps fit well, the canisters are great for storing seeds in over the winter. Just write the type of seed on a piece of masking tape and put it on the side of the canister so you remember what your seeds are.

Joan Bair
Greenville Junction, Maine

A safe, homemade fungicide

I have a trick to stop damping-off disease in my seedlings. I spray the seeds with a garlic spray. Put six cloves in one pint of water and puree in the blender. Strain, then use in a spray bottle.

Judy Ramsay Jensen
San Jose, California

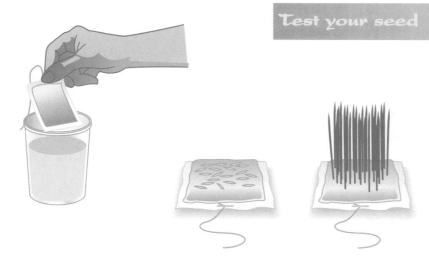

If you're not sure if last year's grass seed is still good or not, try dipping an old, used tea bag a couple of times in a plastic cup filled two-thirds of the way with water. Sprinkle grass seed on the bag and place in a sunny window for a week. Grass will grow if the seed is good.

Mrs. Ruch
Woodbury, New Jersey

Know your seed's needs

Some seeds have special requirements to germinate. Some need light, others need darkness. Some need certain temperatures, and some even need changing temperatures. Know what your seeds need before your plant to avoid disappointment.

WHGC Staff

care and comfort

Jump-start your seeds

Have trouble germinating seeds? Sometimes the toughest ones just sit and don't do anything. To help the really hard-coated seeds germinate, try soaking them overnight in warm water or tea. (The moisture helps to soften the outer seed coat. The acid in the tea does, too.)

Anne Drumm
LaVale, Maryland

Distribute small seeds more easily

When you need to sow small seeds, put them in a large-hole salt or spice container and shake them out where you want them. (It's easier yet if you add some sand or sugar to the seeds in the container.)

Jean Bergin
Mishicot, Wisconsin

Keep your seedlings healthy

To help prevent damping-off diseases when I start seeds, I sterilize the pots and seedling containers by soaking the containers in a solution of one part bleach to nine parts of water for about 10 minutes. After you plant your seeds indoors, cover them with a thin layer of milled sphagnum moss.

Liz Siska
Summit, Illinois

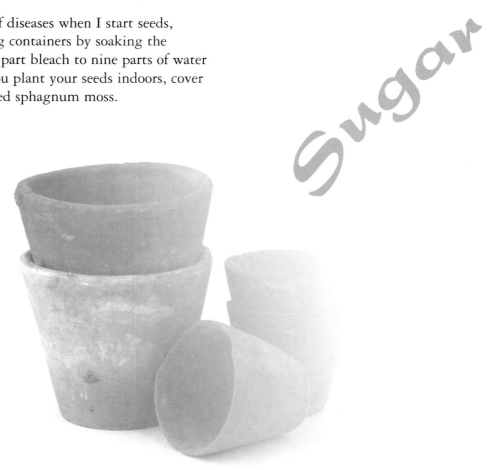

Don't throw away your old seeds. Most stay good for several years, especially if stored in a cool, dry place or freezer. To test your old seeds for viability, lay 10 on a moistened paper towel. Roll up the paper towel and place it in a plastic bag. Move it to a warm place and check in 8 to 10 days. If half the seeds germinate, your rate is about 50 percent, so plant twice as many seeds as usual to make up for the low germination rate.

Walter Chandoha
Annandale, New Jersey

and spice ...

Making mini-greenhouses

I have a trick for mini-greenhouses, while recycling something. When sowing seeds directly into the ground, you can make a mini-greenhouse by covering the area with the clear plastic holders that cakes and muffins come in from the bakery. You can lift them to water every morning and then take them off once the seeds start growing.

Donna Greenbaum
Solana Beach, California

Here's a trick for starting plants from seed. In the area where the days are hot and dry and the evenings are cool, it can be difficult starting plants from seed. The following method has proved to be a successful one, especially in starting tough plants...

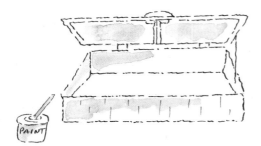

1 Prepare a cold frame by painting the inside and outside white to cut down on the sun's glare.

2 Staple a clear plastic sheet over the top.

3 Lay a sheet along the bottom and up to 2 inches along the inside of the cold frame.

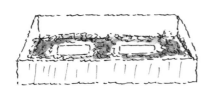

6 Place the flats in a sink or bucket so that they are watered from the bottom and your watering doesn't disturb the seeds. Once the mix is moist, put the flats in the bed of wood shavings in the cold frame.

7 Pour water all around the flats, so you soak the wood shavings. Place a large screen over your cold frame (to keep the shavings moist and shading from the sun).

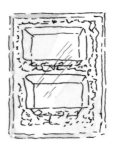

8 To keep heat in once it gets cold, place glass plates over two flats at a time. Avoid leaving the glass on during the day when it's warm or else the flats will get too hot.

ting tough plants...

4 Then add some fluffy wood shavings about 2 inches thick above the plastic lining.

5 In a bucket, lightly moisten a mixture of seed-starting mix. Fill small Kord fiber flats with soil up to a half inch from the top and plant your seeds.

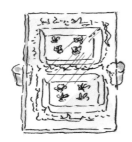

9 As the seedlings grow, raise the glass plates by placing them on small upside down pots.

Once the seedlings have two pair of true leaves, transplant them into 2-inch pots. Place the pots in the bed of wood shavings and soak the wood shavings again. The adjustable cover of plastic on top allows you to control temperature inside.

Reva Kern
Oak Park, California

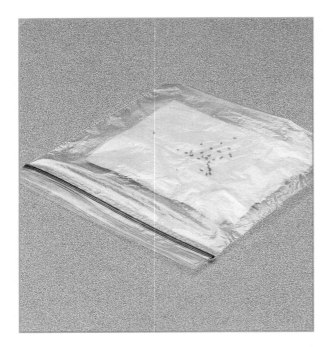

Help your seeds germinate

To germinate seeds easily, soak a paper towel with warm water and gently squeeze the excess water out. Add the seeds on the top half of the paper towel and fold the other half on top of the seeds. Place the paper towel in a sealed baggie and check every three days to see if the seeds have germinated. You can even match the requirements the seeds need—seeds that need dark to germinate are placed in a cabinet; seeds that need light are clipped to my window curtain. After the seeds germinate, they can be removed from the bag and placed into your seed beds, and transplanted after they have two pairs of true leaves. The paper towel decomposes, so you don't have to worry about it.

Vanessa Cadiere
Montegut, Louisiana

Keep them warm

A lot of seeds benefit from a little extra warmth. Starting them on top of a radiator or refrigerator helps speed up germination and helps more seeds germinate.

WHGC Staff

An easy way to distribute seeds

I've recently moved here from England and I have a tip. When planting very fine seeds, mix the seed with very fine sand. This helps you avoid dumping all the seed in one place because the sand is light colored and the seeds are dark. (Plus when the seeds are mixed in the sand you can distribute the seeds over a larger area.) In London I used something we called silver sand; so far I have failed to find it here.

Patricia Ronan
Collierville, Tennessee

Free containers!

You can plant seeds in eggshells filled with compost. Cut a small hole into egg and blow the egg out to use it or just crack the egg in half and use each half as a pot. Poke small holes into the bottom of the egg so that you have water drainage. You can also decorate the eggshells and give them to gardening friends as gifts!

Mary Parnell
Mansfield, Ohio

Save those seeds

You can save money by saving your seeds each year. After the blooms fade, allow the seeds to dry in situ. Gather the dried seed (when it's hard and dry) and store in old plastic bottles, such as medicine bottles. (Your seedlings won't always look like their parents, though; genetics are full of surprises.)

Charles Peckham
Friesland, Wisconsin

Improving *Your Soil*

Soil anchors the garden, providing
the place for plants to lay roots,
as well as the nutrients your
plants need to really thrive.
Simply put, soil is so integral to
gardening success, it's imperative
to pay attention to the problems
that can develop there—whether
it's a lack of nutrients, the
inability to hold or release water,
or bothersome weeds sucking the
soil's richness away from your
desired plants. Everyone needs
help with soil ... here are members' tips for improving it.

g

Time to dig right in...

Don't haul your compost over long distances

Put your compost pile inside of your garden. (You can mask it with tall plants if it doesn't look right.) The nutrients that leach out of the pile will then leach into your garden instead of being wasted. Plus, the compost is right there for easy use!

Sam Burton
North Lauderdale, Florida

A recycled mulch

I save my coffee and tea grounds for my acid-loving plants in the garden. The grounds are organic and add other nutrients to the soil.

Kristi Dulitz
Webster, South Dakota

Hay, there—here is an idea!

I always buy two bales of hay in October for my yard display. I get to use it for a Halloween display, then a fall display and some in my nativity scene in December. I then mulch with the hay from January to March. In March, the hay goes to my compost pile, so there's no waste and five months of use.

Ann Rice
Houston, Texas

Now that's thinking!

We keep our kids' pet ducks and bunnies near our compost pile. When it's time to clean the cages, the compost pile isn't far away and the location makes the hauling easier. Our compost is enriched regularly.

Alice Kennedy
Crawford, Nebraska

Make hay all year long

A new compost idea

I use old coffee grounds in the compost pile. They're good organic matter and composting makes them less acid so you don't have to worry about using them in the garden and changing your soil pH.

Tia Lopez
Boston, New York

Plants need to breathe, too

When you plant or are in the garden, loosen the soil around your plants. Loosening the soil helps get air to the roots so the plants can breathe and then they'll grow faster.

Steve Lacy
Sulligent, Alabama

Go nuts over

A different kind of mulch

As an alternative mulch, try using pecan shell hulls if they're available in your area. The shells are long lasting and look good in the garden, plus they're organic.

Barbara Melton
Alvarado, Texas

Plant up

For really wet spots, or in areas with heavy rains or clay soils, plant in raised beds. The additional height adds drainage and you can use different kinds of soil in the beds. Our vegetable garden survived the heavy May rains much better after we planted in raised beds.

Norma Hosea
Scottsburg,
Indiana

Add organic matter to your soil

Dig a mixture of potato peelings and crushed eggshells into the dirt around your roses for a healthier plant.

Mary Crites
Farmington, Missouri

Let nature compost for you

During the winter, instead of throwing out my potato peelings, coffee grounds and other plant-type kitchen scraps, I scatter them in the garden and till them into the ground in spring when the ground thaws.

Mary Santaw
North Troy, Vermont

A great mulching idea

Overlap sections of newspapers under an inch or two of mulch for the ultimate in weed control.

Susie Yates
Midland, Texas

A blender recipe

Quicker composting

To accelerate the composting process of my vegetable and fruit scraps, I place the scraps into a plastic bag that I put into the freezer compartment of my refrigerator for a few days. The liquids of the scraps freeze and expands the pores of the materials. I put the frozen scraps into my compost pile and the ice melts, leaving more spaces for the bacteria to begin decomposing the scraps. You could also put the frozen scraps in the blender to make composting even faster.

Leonard Bykowski
Henderson, Nevada

Whip up some compost

I grind up my kitchen scraps—no meat or grease—in my kitchen blender with a little water. Then I pour this pre-compost into my garden. It's a fast and easy way to provide essential nutrients directly to the plants.

Anna Vonschwerdtner
Upper Marlboro, Maryland

Not a rotten idea

For adding some organic matter into your soil, bury a rotting log in the bed. (Don't worry if you see some mushrooms growing, though.)

Cheryl McAtee
Vancouver,
Washington

Compost in winter

In the summer, I bury all of my vegetable scraps in an open area of the garden. When autumn comes, I dig a hole big enough for a five-gallon bucket that I've cut the bottom out of. Pack loose dirt around the outside of the bucket and put an old hubcap or something over the top of the bucket. In the winter, I have a place to put my vegetable scraps because my compost pile is frozen. In spring, dig the bucket out and bury the scraps with dirt. In no time, it'll be composted.

Lucille Norris
Bartlett, Nebraska

Leave your leaves

When harvesting your rhubarb, pull the stalks off. Detach the leaf from the stalk (the leaf is poisonous anyway) and lay the leaf on the ground below the plant. It works as a nice mulch and keeps dirt from splashing onto the other stems.

Arella Emery
Sturgis, Michigan

Winter mulch

Save the long needles dropped from long-needled evergreens, such as white pines. They make wonderful blanket covers for the winter protection of spring flower beds. You can also scatter the needles between garden rows to discourage weed growth and prevent your shoes from getting muddy.

Roxie Stahl
Huntington, Indiana

Save organic materials

When you dig up a new area of ground, save the old roots of plants that you dig up. You can put them into the compost bin. Using the compost will help to cut down on weeds in the future.

Ruth Ann Oliver
Marion, Indiana

A low-cost compost bin

Quick and easy compost bins

Here is a tip for everyone who would like to make a compost bin but doesn't have money for one of the fancy ones. Watch the newspapers to find sales on plastic trash cans. Look for a good one with a tight-fitting lid. If it has wheels, you can move your bin across the yard easily. Black cans are great because they hold the heat of the compost well. All you have to do is turn the can upside down and drill some holes in the bottom to allow excess water to drain away. Then drill a ring of holes every 6 inches up from the bottom to the top. Drill the holes in the ring about 3 inches apart. Now you have a handy, low-cost compost bin. If you have more than one bin, you can turn your compost easily by moving it from one can to the next.

Mary Beth Abordo
Kelseyville, California

Tool
Essentials

Gardening's most important tool
may well be your imagination.
But to make your dreams come true
takes some hard work—and beyond
your hands, a variety of tools can
make individual gardening tasks
much easier. So here are members'
techniques and tips for getting the
most out of your tools (to save time
and energy), and even create some
tools of your own...a variety of tool
essentials to make gardening easier,
more efficient and even more
enjoyable.

Make your tools work even harder...

Easy plant markers

There's a good way to make garden labels without buying the expensive ones from the stores. What I do is use white plastic knives (the kind used at summer picnics) and write on them with permanent marker. All you have to do is push the handle into the soil and you have a great label.

Amy Sneeden
Lake Norden, South Dakota

Special package

For an easy, convenient place to store small hand tools, string, scissors, labels, plant ties and other useful things, put an old mailbox next to the garden gate. You always know where they are then and they're nice and close for all those spontaneous garden chores.

Jack Mabry
Benton, Kentucky

Make a drip watering system

An easy and economical form of drip watering: With a utility knife, cut off the bottom of an empty plastic 1 liter liquor bottle and remove the pourer, but save the lid. Using a heavy hammer or sledge, drive a 3- to 4-foot length of metal pipe at least 18 inches into the ground and rotate the top of the pipe vigorously to create a V-shaped hole to accept the neck of the bottle. Remove the pipe and insert the bottle, neck down. Drill a hole in the top of the lid and replace on the bottle for drip watering. You can leave the lid off if you want. You can also spray-paint the bottles for more visibility.

Mil Hyde
Drasco, Arkansas

Empty your hoses

This might seem like a small tip, but it really made a big difference in my gardening work. I have a really large yard, so I have to have a very long water hose to irrigate with. I've found that when I have to drag it from one area to the other to water a new planting or whatever, it is much easier to move if the hose is empty. It weighs much less and is more flexible.

Beverle Sweitzer
Silver Spring, Maryland

Old nylon stockings are great as plant ties. You can tie tomato plants to a fence or other support because the nylon stretches and doesn't choke the plant as the stems grow bigger.

Joanne Drake
Saint Petersburg,
Florida

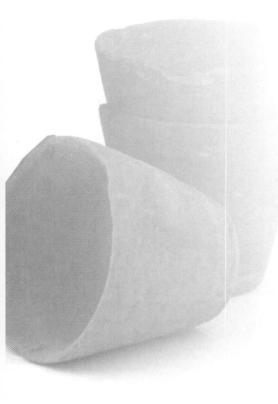

Plant screening

I have another use for old pantyhose: Cut them into small sections and use the sections to line the bottom of your pots. They keep the soil in, but let water out (and keep bugs out, too).

Beverly Baustian
Camden, Arizona

When you have some heavy digging to do, a digging fork can make the job much easier than a regular shovel.

Anna Summerhays
Salt Lake City, Utah

Put things away

One of the best habits you can have is to always put your tools away in the same place after you use them. That way, you never have to go looking for them and it is easy to explain where they are to someone else.

WHGC Staff

Plant markers

For nice and inexpensive plant markers, I recycle my quart-sized yogurt tubs. Simply cut vertical strips from the sides of the tub and write the name of the plant and other information you need on the strips with permanent marker. Stick them in the ground and you've got nice markers.

Cheryl Alexander
Cottonwood, Arizona

I use old, run pantyhose to store bulbs in that I have to dig up before winter. You can make a knot between each bulb so that air flows and if one rots, the others won't. You can hang them easily, too.

L.B. Stephens
Kirkland, Washington

Store your

Remember to recycle

Cat lovers can recycle the white, plastic gallon jugs that some brands of cat litter come in. (Scoop-Away is one brand.) Just cut up the sides of the jug for plant labels of whatever size you need. Write on them with a permanent marker for season-long information.

Diane Taylor Hayes
Greer, South Carolina

More permanent labels

When you make plant labels, the ink often fades away. I use an enamel paint pen to write on my garden stakes. It stays on better than permanent ink.

Sue Cerny
St. Johns, Michigan

You can use kids' old, discarded toboggans to pull around tools or plants in your garden. They pull easily over grass, especially when it's wet. If you want to, you can also dig them down into the soil and plant in them to make shallow containers.

Peggy Flanders
Syracuse,
New York

bulbs in nylons

Flag it

When starting plants indoors in trays, I've found the best and cheapest way to keep all the information I need about the seeds is to use a Post-it Note. What I do is cut the sticky end of the Post-it Note off, write what I need on it and then fold it over the toothpick.

Diana Woods
Boise, Idaho

I've found a way to recycle those cans that frozen concentrated juices come in. I cut the metal bottom off and put the cardboard part of the can over my newly set-out transplants (such as tomatoes, cabbage, peppers, etc.) to keep the cutworms off of my plants.

*Ernestine Cartwright
Cookeville, Tennessee*

A great way to conserve water is to use soaker hoses and drippers. We must not abuse water.

*Edward Harwood
Ludington,
Michigan*

Here's a great way to recycle and make plant labels. All you have to do is cut up the old or leftover slats from plastic mini-blinds (when you shorten the blinds, you have extra slats, too). Cut the slats into the lengths of your choice and then cut one end into a point so that you can stick it into the soil. Use a permanent marker to label your plants.

Kathy Johnson
Tuscumbia, Alabama

You can recycle large containers that your trees and shrubs come in before you plant them. Cut the bottom off and slit the side open so it can be put around trees as a border to keep grass or weeds out.

Diana Woods
Boise, Idaho

Re-use old miniblinds

I have an inexpensive way to control or confine plants that grow tall instead of staking them. Use rings. Buy the 42-inch high tomato rings and cut them with wire cutters just above the lower ring. This gives you two different sized rings to use for different plants.

Sharon Blodgett
Wenatchee, Washington

I save and recycle each of my throw-away miniature Christmas tree light strings after Christmas. You can use the strings for plant tie-ups or for making small trellises.

Dixie Lemay
Oroville,
Washington

Quick clean up

A shop vac makes cleaning up fallen crab apples or similar garden debris a quick and easy job.

Jeannie Burns
Endicott, Wisconsin

Use shop vacuum for

Strong stakes

I use rebar (any type of metal) to stake my plants on. I use them individually. I put wire overhead in a criss-cross fashion (use ordinary small gauge tie wire). I tie flagging over the wire. This helps to partially shade my plants from the hot sun and the flagging blows around and helps to keep birds out of the garden.

Sam Standerfer
Kingman, Arizona

When I go out to weed my garden, I like to bring an old, plastic laundry basket with me. I can weed and put the weeds inside. The basket is lightweight, even when it's full, and the holes in the side allow the excess dirt to sift out and go back to the garden.

Caroline Beatty
Prentiss, Mississippi

apple pickin'

Trellis idea

Instead of buying a wooden trellis for our clematis, we bought some 150-pound fishing line. The line can be woven in and out and it makes the vines look like they're suspended in the air. Plus, it's less expensive.

Barb Kropaczewski
Perrysburg, Ohio

The most interesting trellis around

If you live near the woods, you can find really unique tree branches to stick in the ground for growing morning glories or other vines. I've built a trellis with branches and wire fencing to train vines.

Rose DeLuca
Bausman,
Pennsylvania

That's what it's for

I invested in a bulb auger attachment for my cordless drill to make bulb planting less of a chore. It worked great; I planted 100 bulbs in an hour. It was so easy, and the best investment I've made in gardening. You can also drill holes for planting plants. It's great.

Joyce Mills
Ashland, Virginia

Attach a bulb auger

To stake early peas in a small garden, use chicken wire along each row. Put stakes in along each plant to hold the wire up. The peas grow up the wire and are very easy to pick. Once pea season is done, you can just take the fencing down.

Virginia Beesmer
Kingston, New York

to drill

Tool carrier

To save your back when you carry around a sprayer or lots of large tools, try using a golf bag cart. It's much easier to pull around and holds just about everything you need.

Lora Redweik
Twelve Mile, Indiana

You can make a splint for broken plant parts with a plastic drinking straw. This is especially good for small plants. Cut a 3- to 4-inch piece off of a straw and slice the straw open lengthwise. Wrap the straw around the broken plant and seal with tape.

*Darlene Reinoehl
Klingerstown,
Pennsylvania*

Supports

Tomato cages have other uses than tomatoes. You can use the cages over your rose bushes or other perennial plants to help them maintain their shape and to help support the blooms when it rains.

*Paul Bardelmeier
Saint Louis,
Missouri*

A carpet of carpet

You can recycle old carpet by cutting it into strips and laying it down in between beds to control weeds. It really keeps the weeds down. You may also spray some pre-emergent herbicide on the bottom for additional control.

*Leonard Duroche
Minneapolis, Minnesota*

Tomato cages and glads

Sometimes gladiolas flop over in the summer. To prevent this from happening, plant the gladiolas in a circle and place a tomato cage around that area. This will give the glads support when flowering. (If you paint the cages light green, they'll be less obvious, too.)

Lynette Gelling
Clayton, Wisconsin

Watering windowboxes

I have windowboxes at my lake cottage. Since I'm only there on the weekends, keeping the windowboxes watered is a problem. I use an eight ounce water bottle to hold water and bury it in the back corner of my box. Then I run a wick from a hole I poked near the top of the bottle and run it the length of the box between the layers of soil between the bottom of the box and the rootballs of my flowers. Each weekend I water the box and fill the water bottles to hold them over until the next weekend.

Kim Neuhauser
Leesburg, Indiana

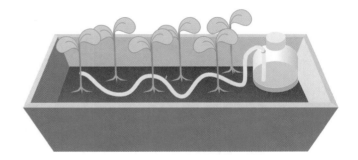

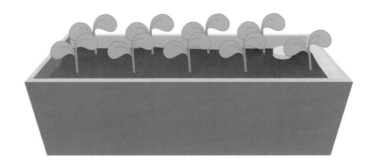

Keep your tools clean

Carry a bucket of anti-bacterial solution (such as a half cup of bleach or alcohol in a gallon of water) around with you in the garden. You can dip your tools into it when pruning to help prevent the spread of disease, or you can put your cuttings in it for a short time before planting them.

Phyllis Downing
Rose City,
Michigan

Don't chop down small trees

I had an 8-foot tree die during a storm. I could have cried, but being an optimist, I looked at it and thought it could have another use as a stake. I put weedblock and five 12-inch pots of soil around the tree. I tied three to four strong cords per pot around the outside and attached the ends to marked limbs. It makes a great trellis for beans, cucumbers, morning glories or other vines.

Teresa Penrod
Wilmington, North Carolina

Support your morn

Morning glories on the side

Would you like to grow morning glories, but just don't have a support? Try running a garden string up the gutter for morning glories or other small vines to climb. You can hold the strings down by tying them to a rock. They'll wind up and climb to the top of the house.

Janine Sarnowski
Seville, Ohio

To stake my tomatoes, I use 8-foot lengths of reinforcing rod with a half inch diameter. You can drive them about a foot into the ground so they're sturdy for your tomatoes to climb on. The stakes won't rot away, so you can use them for many, many years.

Brian Brown
Pacific, Missouri

ing glories

You can recycle old window screens. If they get a rip or can't be used for other reasons, lay them on the soil to form small protective covers for new seedlings or newly planted seeds.

Joan Zora
Mount Prospect, Illinois

Need markers to remember what rows you've planted what in? Go and laminate your old, empty seed packets and punch a hole at the top and bottom to place on a stake (or tie it to the stake). They're ready to use as garden markers, and you can use them year after year.

Sally Olson
Hayden, Idaho

Stake your rows

Special blossoms

I have a fun tip for tying up perennials. I'm always on the hunt at craft stores for rolls of ribbon at close-out prices in the colors of my blossoming plants. I use the narrow 1/4- to 1/2- inch ribbon to tie the stalks up the support canes. I tie them off with little bows. It adds color and interest to the plant. From a distance, it looks as though the blossom color is evident from the bottom of the plant up.

Nancy Freeman
Menasha, Wisconsin

Transplanting seedlings in the spring can be tough because the seedlings are so tender. I find that my bulb digger is an excellent tool when transplanting seedlings in the spring because it makes the job easier.

Dorothy Leitner
Saint Paul,
Minnesota

I re-use the plastic packs that annual seedlings come in from the nursery. If you fill them with soil and place mum cuttings in them, the cuttings root by autumn and allow you to add some extra color once fall comes.

Arvin Stems
Cedars Grove, New Jersey

To help keep track of hand tools that sometimes get inadvertently left laying around (especially if you have kids helping you or you get easily side-tracked), paint the handles at least partially down and all the way around with a bright fluorescent day-glo paint that's easily spotted. To increase visibility, it helps to apply a flat white base coat under your color. It takes less of the colored paint, too. The flat white undercoat really enhances the brightness.

C.A. Thompson
Little Corners, Pennsylvania

Comfortable cold frame

I like to make small greenhouses for starting seeds or cuttings. Here's how: When buying a throw or comforter, save the zipped plastic bag it comes in. Make a frame to fit inside the bag out of bamboo or other stakes (cut them to the right size) and secure them with electrical or duct tape. (The frame keeps the shape of the bag so that it doesn't collapse and the zipper allows you to control the amount of air circulation you have.) They work wonderfully for me—almost all of my propagated plants were propagated from this method.

Tammy Quan
Avila Beach, California

Attractive and useful

I have a great way to make little plant markers. I bought wooden craft spoons from the arts and crafts department of our local store. The spoons come in a package of many spoons for a low cost (mine was a package of 75 spoons for only $1.89). There is plenty of room to write information on the spoons and they are attractive and a lot cheaper than the commercial markers you see in garden stores.

J. Emonds
Worcester, Massachusetts

Wooden spoons

Make your own soil

I use a portable cement mixer to mix dirt, compost and horse and cow manure when I'm making a new flower bed.

Philip Cobin
Ferguson, Missouri

Temporary protection

You can cut the bottom off of a two-liter plastic soda bottle. When you get new plants in the mail or set out new transplants, plant the plants and put the soda bottle over the plant. You can leave the cap on or off, depending on how sunny it is outside. When your plant is established, take the mini-greenhouse off. (For longer, shorter greenhouses to protect seedlings, you can cut the bottles in half lengthwise, too.)

Sue Macyszyn
Browns Mills, New Jersey

The many uses of plastic

I use plastic cross-stitch sheets (that you can get from most craft stores—I like to wait until they're on sale) in the garden. I line the bottom of my pots with the material instead of using little stones or pottery shards to help keep the soil from draining out. I also use the plastic sheets to tie vining plants to my deck. The vines can climb on the sheets until they're large enough to climb on their own.

Judy Somers
Saline, Michigan

I make homemade mini-greenhouses for sprouting seeds or rooting leaves and other cuttings. Each greenhouse is made of two saucers, one smaller than the other, and a straight sided glass jar or bowl. The smaller saucer should fit inside of the larger, and be filled with about a half inch of vermiculite. You can insert the cuttings, leaves or seeds in the vermiculite and cover with the glass jar. The jar should fit in between the small and large saucers. It helps keeps water from condensing and running down the side of the jar onto the table. It is also easy to move the mini-greenhouse if you need to.

Lois Vennewitz
Marine-on-Saint-Croix,
Minnesota

I use easy-to-make plant guards to protect newly set out transplants from sun, wind and late frosts. The guards are made from scrap pieces of corrugated fiberglass and ¾- by ¾-inch cedar. The length or width of the fiberglass is not critical, just that it's large enough to protect your plants. To make a guard, roll up the ends, lap one corrugation, clamp and tape. Drill two holes through the fiberglass. Select a cedar stake about 4 inches longer than the height of the fiberglass. Position the stake in the lapped corrugation and secure it. The fiberglass of the guard will transmit adequate light for transplants and shields the plant from excessive sun and wind, as well as pests. If a frost is forecasted, drape a piece of fabric over the top.

Victor McHenry
Hot Springs, Arkansas

Keep your gloves ready

At the end of the day, gardening gloves can get pretty dirty, and sometimes pretty wet. To ensure the gloves will be dry for the next day, I attach a few snap clothes pins to the door jam of my garden shed. The gloves never get lost and get a chance to air-dry for work the next morning.

Dorothy Raimond
Anderson, South Carolina

From ladder to trellis

I found an old ladder at an auction. Some of the wrungs were cracked so I couldn't use it. Then I decided I could use it as a lattice for my clematis. It looks great.

Marjorie Montney
Allentown, Michigan

Homemade obelisks

I have an inexpensive substitute for an English gardening obelisk. I use one vinyl-coated tomato cage and one round cage. I bent the bottom ribs of the round cage and taped the two together. Then I used twine to make supports for the vine and taped the round cage securely to the bottom one.

Vinyl Walker
Ontario, Oregon

Easy on the hands

Does using garden tools give you blisters after a hard day? I found a way to make the jobs in the garden easier on my hands. I use the foam handles made for bicycle handlebars on my garden tools to help reduce the blisters and stress on my hands. The handles are inexpensive and can be bought at department stores or bike shops.

Robin Nordstrom
Ellettsville, Indiana

You can recycle your old egg cartons and other small cardboard containers for planting seeds. They work great and can be put right out into the garden because they degrade. (You can't do this with Styrofoam containers, though, only cardboard.) I also recycle plastic containers (such as margarine tubs) for plants by poking holes in the bottom and using the lid as a nice saucer.

Carrol Ann Webb
Petaluma,
California

The scissor-type dog-poo scoop works great for picking up leaves and other debris from the garden. There's no need for back stress caused by bending over to pick things up.

Gail Barnhill
Tucson, Arizona

The clear plastic bags that you get from the dry cleaners can be recycled into mini-greenhouses. Make a cylinder of chicken wire big enough to cover your plant to be protected, but still leaving enough space for more growth. Cover the sides of the chicken wire with the bags and tie them on. As days get warmer, remove the greenhouses and replace them about an hour before sunset. If the weather gets really cold, invert a cardboard carton over the greenhouse.

WHGC Staff

Before you have to dig a number of holes, take a laundry marker and mark the handle of your hand mattock in one-half inch increments up to 12 or 18 inches. This gives you a quick and easy measuring stick for gauging hole depths.

Dennis Campbell
Monroe, North Carolina

I think I can

I am a small-built person with five acres of gardens. Some friends gave me a red wagon to use in the garden because a wheelbarrow was too hard to maneuver.

Michele Mendez
North Fort Myers,
Florida

Quick and easy cold frames

Hot glue some clear plastic over old table rims, door frames, waterbed boxes and so on, and then lean them against the south side of any building. Glue a couple of plastic bags on the side and you have a portable cold frame for hardening off plants.

Steve Adamson
Maricopa, Arizona

I've found a great use for a cracked aquarium: I can start seeds inside. Place the seeds in pots and set them in the tank. Stack egg cartons at various heights to raise or lower the pots. Watering is a breeze. I've even attached a grow light to a board and hung it over the top. (It also makes a good terrarium.)

Cris Samuel
Lexington, South Carolina

Special supports

Put those old wire hangers in your closets to good use. I take a heavy wire cutters and unwind the wire from the neck of a metal hanger. I then stretch the hanger out straight, and using the cutters, bend the crooked neck of the hanger horizontally. Just stick the hanger in the ground next to tall lilies, gladiolas and so on, and curl the crook of the wire into a semi-circle, just enough to hold the stem. They're just flexible enough to give the flowers a natural look without being too stiff, and best of all, they are even less noticeable after they rust.

Ross Cooper
Shelbyville, Tennessee

A great garden tool

As you put your garden to bed this year, you'll want to trim back old growth from some plants, such as iris, or the spent blooms from flowers such as candytuft. I've found that using an old, serrated knife for the job makes the cleanup much easier.

Audrey Mather
Roseburg, Oregon

Seedy shoes

To help with my direct seeding, I glue an old slip-on shoe to a square of plywood (cut off the plywood to a size equal to your ride-row width). At seeding time, place it on your foot to "hug" the seedbed and level the row for secure germination. My board is 12 inches by 18 inches so I can tamp two sizes of row.

Carol Perzy
Litchfield, Ohio

Tag 'em

Keep the plant tags that come with your plants. You can tape them in a notebook so you have a record of what you've planted and what conditions the plants like.

WHGC Staff

Hanging tools

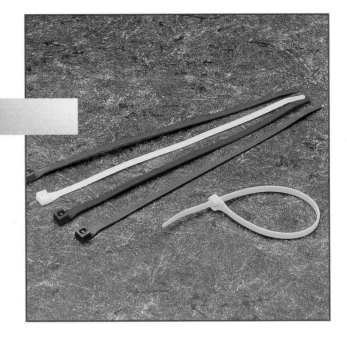

To help keep track of your trowels and other hand-tools, pick up a few plastic cable ties at any auto parts store. (These are rigid plastic ties about 6 inches long and a half of an inch wide.) Hook these ties in a circle through the hole on the end of your tool and you have a handy, non-corrosive loop to slip around a nail or hook when you hang up your tool.

Eileen Gieser
Orange, California

Save your knees

I cut the legs of an old pair of my husband's blue jeans to make shorts for him. However, the "leg" part of the jeans was still good. I had a piece of foam rubber just the right size to fit in one of the jean legs, so I stuffed it in and then closed the two outside seams with my sewing machine. Presto! A sturdy, comfortable kneeling pad to use outside in my garden.

Penny Kipley
Traverse City, Michigan

I recycle the Cd-rom disks that internet providers mail out. What I do is tie string through the holes in the centers of the disks and hang them from a fence or stake. They'll dangle in the breeze and reflect light. The reflected light helps scare away deer and birds from my garden.

Jodie Stevenson
Export,
Pennsylvania

Early springtime salads

I like to get an early start on my salads, so I take a large pot filled with soil and sprinkle my lettuce seeds on it, then wet it down. I use a piece of clear plastic, at least two to three times the size of the top of the pot to cover the pot. I tie a string around it to hold the plastic down. If it's a warm day after the seedlings emerge, remove the plastic, but put it back on at night.

Shirley Pennington
Ironton, Missouri

Overwintering tender bulbs

I save the mesh bags that produce is bagged in at the grocery store to store my tender bulbs that need to be lifted in the fall. The mesh helps keep air flowing around the bulbs so I have less problem with rot.

Karen Evers
Jackson, Mississippi

Special screening

I place a piece of window screen at the bottom of my containers to prevent insects from getting in and soil from getting out.

Scott Sterling
Imperial, Pennsylvania

Keep those containers

I recycle the plastic pots that my perennials, trees and shrubs come in. They make quick and easy covers for plants if a frost is predicted. I also use them to cover plants when I dump mulch into the garden—then I don't have to uncover any plants, I just pull up the pot. They're great, too, for sharing plants.

Sharon Parish
Franklin, Indiana

Screen out insects

A tool in disguise

For weeding between paving blocks or small spaces in the garden, use a shrimp cleaner. The tool is inexpensive from the store. The inside angle of the device also has a cutting edge and the angle makes it easy on your wrist to use.

P.C. Diedrich
Chicago, Illinois

I use wooden chopsticks to mark where I've planted bulbs and herbaceous perennials. When they're dormant, I know where they are so I don't disturb them or accidentally pull them. The chopsticks don't look bad in the garden, either.

W. David Haggarty
Davis, California

Bulb collars

To remember where bulbs are at the end of the season, cut 3-inch circles of plastic from two-liter plastic soda bottles. Sink them in the ground just below the soil line. You can dig around in the soil and know where your bulbs are without having to dig them up or have markers sticking up when they're dormant.

Sharon Mirtaheri
Germantown, Maryland

A great tool

Use an old kitchen knife in the garden. It's great for weeding fibrous-rooted plants (cut the soil beneath the root system), pruning or dead-heading and for cutting flowers.

WHGC Staff

X marks the spot

If you forget what your perennials look like or plant new ones in the fall, mark where they are. That way, when spring comes and the plants come up, you won't accidentally pull them up as weeds. If you mark them with labels, you'll always remember what they are, too.

Debbie Pompeii
Struthers, Ohio

Recycling stir sticks

Need plant markers or small stakes? When you clean up after a painting project, save the paint stirring sticks. They work great.

Dale Ann Kelly
Levittown, New York

Seed collecting tip

To collect seeds at the end of the season, cut about 8 inches off the end of an old pair of pantyhose and then pull this "mitten" over the stem and seeds you want. Secure the sock by tying it on with another piece of nylon. That way, if the seeds "pop" off the plant before you can get to them, you'll still have them in your sock.

Shirley Lightkep
Ambler, Pennsylvania

Sweet pepper supports

When your peppers get heavy with fruit, the branches sometimes break. If you plant the peppers in tomato cages, the branches will be supported enough that they don't break.

WHGC Staff

Vegetable
Secrets

Vegetables seem to comprise a
gardening league all their own.
We get to see and smell the fruits of
our labors (who can argue that a
red, ripe tomato on the vine isn't
pleasing to both the eyes and the
nose?). We also get to taste the
rewards (fresh, home-grown
produce is a tastebud experience
unmatched). So here are plenty of
ideas, straight from members'
gardens, to help you enjoy all the
eye-, ear- and tastebud-pleasures
that vegetables bring ... true secrets
to vegetable gardening success.

Make your garden even tastier.

Staggered plantings

Plant short rows of beans at frequent intervals to keep your harvest small and stretched over a longer period.

WHGC Staff

Tomato trick

The Infrared Plastic Mulch (IRT) helped me produce more tomatoes and peppers in my vegetable garden and helped warm the soil earlier. It is available from some mail-order catalogs.

Louis Schoenhorn
Fairfield, Connecticut

Warm up your

Vine-ripened tomatoes

A week before frost, pull up your entire tomato plant with the fruit still attached and hang it by the roots in a cool, frost-free area. The tomatoes will ripen and have full flavor. The warmer the area, the faster they'll ripen.

WHGC Staff

Fresh parsley—even in winter!

In early July, fill 4-inch pots with a compost, sand and peat moss mixture, then sink into the ground. Plant your parsley in the pots and water. Two weeks after the seeds sprout, thin to two seedlings per pot. Before frost, dig up the pots and bring them inside to a sunny window. You'll have parsley all winter.

*Walter Chandoha
Annandale,
New Jersey*

garden

Get a head start

If you want bigger onions, garlic and shallots, plant the sets indoors in plastic six-packs about a month ahead of time. Fill the partitions with a moistened mix of equal parts of compost, peat moss and sand. Insert the sets half way into the mix and place in a sunny window or sheltered porch. Warmth and moisture will trigger the growth of your bulbs. When the weather permits, plant them outdoors.

WHGC Staff

For more pollination

Plant your corn in blocks of 4 to 6 short rows instead of 2 to 3 long rows. This increases pollination of your corn, as corn is usually pollinated by the wind. To keep your corn harvests going, stagger some plantings every 2 to 3 weeks.

WHGC Staff

Garden coolers

To help start your season earlier, or if you want to prolong the season in autumn, cover your tomato plants with Styrofoam coolers. The coolers will help insulate them and prevent them from freezing.

Mrs. Schlichting
Frohna, Missouri

Little buddies

When I plant beet and other vegetables that take longer than a week to come up, I sow a few radishes along the row so I can hoe the weeds and not the small plants as they come up.

Robert & Alice Hegemann
Fremont, Nebraska

Broccoli times two

After harvesting a head of broccoli, don't remove the plant. Below where the central head was harvested, smaller heads will begin to grow from each node. Side dress the plant with some 10-10-10 fertilizer. Your chance of getting a good second crop is better in the fall because in spring the weather gets warm as summer approaches and the heads are more likely to go to flower.

Walter Chandoha
Annandale, New Jersey

Removable supports

When we put out our pole beans, we put up 5-foot posts 5 to 6 feet apart and put two by four wire fencing along the row about 4 inches off the ground. We plant our beans on each side of the fencing. They're much easier to pick this way, and the fence can be rolled up for next year once the beans are done.

Allene Degenhardt
Percy, Illinois

Light leeks

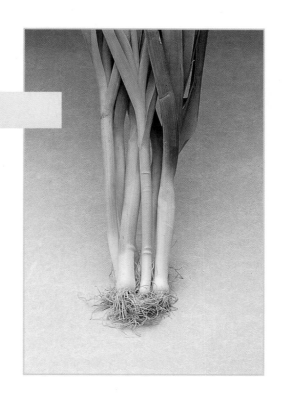

Instead of mounding dirt around the bottom of my leeks to make the stem white and tender, I stack straw around each one and then cover the straw with boards. This keeps the leeks much cleaner than using dirt.

*John Megyesi
Huron, Ohio*

fruit

Get more veggies

To lengthen the vegetable season in Zone 8 and 9 gardens, a shadecloth of burlap, along with drip irrigation and judicious pruning, can be used to produce early fall fruit on peppers and tomatoes.

*James Flagg
Sugar Land, Texas*

Three sisters

Native Americans were adept at growing produce from the land. One of their practices was to plant the "three sisters." To do this yourself, make a mound of soil and plant corn, bean and squash seeds in the mound. If you stagger the plantings properly, the beans will grow up the corn stalks and be harvested before the corn was ripe. The squash would shade the mound, preserving soil moisture and reducing weeds for the beans and corn. The squash would ripen for the traditional fall harvest.

Robert Hunter
Middlebury, Connecticut

Special seed mix

I used to have trouble seeding my carrots evenly. Then I discovered a trick. Mix them with coffee grounds and peat moss—the seedlings just love it.

Kate Barnett
Santa Cruz,
California

Add a little color

There are purple kinds of asparagus—they taste just as good and add a striking visual element to the vegetable garden. Combine the plants with bronze fennel for a distinct, airy appearance.

WHGC Staff

Companion buddies

I plant my lettuce in between my rows of squash. The squash vines shade the lettuce to keep it cool so it bolts later in the year. Plus, I save space in the garden so I have more room for other plants.

Janiene Oliver
Golden, Colorado

Rows of turf?

Design your vegetable garden with strips of lawn between strips of garden soil where you plant the vegetables. Instead of tilling the aisles between the rows to keep weeds down, you can set up a permanent lawn to mow. It's much easier to mow grass than till soil. The grass strips can be any size, as long as they fit your lawn mower. I make mine at least twice the mower width to accommodate any vegetables that might hang out over the grass.

Sharon Schwardt
Saint James, Minnesota

Plant Societies

Plant and gardening societies offer gardeners an opportunity to learn more about gardening in general and specific plants in detail, both from publications and from spending time with other gardeners.

The American Dianthus Society
Rand B. Lee, President
P. O. Box 22232
Santa Fe, NM 87502-2232
randbear@nets.com
Annual Dues $15

American Fern Society
Dr. Richard Hauk
456 McGill Place
Atlanta, GA 30312
Annual dues $8

American Hemerocallis Society
Elly Launius, Secretary
1454 Rebel Drive
Jackson, MS 39211
Annual dues $18

American Horticultural Society
Alexandria, VA 22308-1300
oliverahs@aol.com
Annual dues $35

American Hosta Society
Robyn Duback
7802 NE 63rd Street
Vancouver, WA 98662
giboshiman@aol.com
Annual dues $19

American Iris Society
Marilyn R. Harlow,
Membership Secretary
P. O. Box 8455
San Jose, CA 95155-8455
103262.1512@compuserve.com
Annual dues $18

Sections of AIS include:
Dwarf Iris Society of America
Historic Iris Preservation Society
Louisiana Iris Society of America
The Reblooming Iris Society

The Society for Japanese Irises
Society for Pacific Native Iris
Society for Siberian Irises
Species Iris Group of
    North America
Spuria Iris Society

American Penstemon Society
Ann W. Bartlett,
Membership Secretary
1569 South Holland Court
Lakewood, CO 80232
Annual dues $10

American Peony Society
Greta Kessenich
250 Interlachen Road
Hopkins, MN 55343
Annual dues $7.50

American Primrose, Primula & Auricula
Society
Addaline W. Robinson
9705 SE Spring Crest Drive
Portland, OR 97225
Annual dues $20

American Rock Garden Society
P. O. Box 67
Millwood, NY 10546
Annual dues $25

Cottage Garden Society
5 Nixon Close, Thornhill
Dewsbury, West Yorkshire
England WR12 OJA
Annual dues $20

The Flower and Herb Exchange
Diane Whealy
3076 North Winn Road
Decorah, IA 52101
Annual dues $5

Hardy Fern Foundation
P. O. Box 166
Medina, WA 98039-0166
Annual dues $20

The Hardy Plant Society
Mrs. Pam Adams
Little Orchard, Great Comberton
Pershore, Worcestershire
England WR10 3DP

Hardy Plant Society of Oregon
Julie Maudlin, Membership Chair
2148 Summit Drive
Lake Oswego, OR 97034
Annual dues $20

International Violet Association
Elaine Kudela
8604 Main Road
Berlin Heights, OH 44814-9620
Annual dues $15

Los Angeles International Fern Society
P. O. Box 90943
Pasadena, CA 91109-0943
Annual dues $20

National Chrysanthemum Society
Galen L. Goss
10107 Homar Pond Drive
Fairfax Station, VA 22039-1650
Annual dues $12.50

Northwest Perennial Alliance
Ann Bucher, NPA Chair
P. O. Box 45574, University Station
Seattle, WA 98145
Annual dues $15

Sources for Plants, Seeds and Supplies

Vegetable and Flower Seeds

Burpee Seeds
300 Park Avenue
Warminster, PA 18974
800-888-1447

Cook's Garden
P.O. Box 535
Londonderry, VT 05148
802-824-3400

Johnny's Selected Seeds
Foss Hill Road
Albion, ME 04910
207-437-4301

Nichols Garden
Nursery
1190 North Pacific
Hwy.
Albany, OR 97321
541-928-9280

Park Seed
1 Parkton Ave.
Greenwood, SC 29647
800-845-3369

Pinetree Garden Seeds
P.O. Box 300
New Gloucester, ME
04260
207-926-3400

Shepherd's Garden
Seeds
30 Irene St.
Torrington, CT 06790
860-482-3638

Perennials and Shrubs

Bluestone Perennials
7213 Middle Ridge Rd.
Madison, OH 44057
800-852-5243

Carroll Gardens
444 E. Main St.
Westminster, MD
21157
800-638-6334

Joy Creek Nursery
20300 N.W. Watson
Road
Scappoose, OR 97056
503-543-7474

Klehm Nursery
4210 N. Duncan Rd.
Champaign, IL 61821
800-553-3715

Milaeger's Gardens
4838 Douglas Ave.
Racine, WI 53402
800-669-9956

Niche Gardens
111 Dawson Road
Chapel Hill, NC 27516
919-967-0078

Siskiyou Rare Plant
Nursery
2825 Cummings Road
Medford, OR 97501
503-772-6846

Andre Viette Nursery
Rt. 1, Box 16
Fishersville, VA 22939
703-942-2118

Wayside Gardens
1 Garden Lane
Hodges, SC 26965
800-845-1124

White Flower Farm
P.O. Box 50
Litchfield, CT 06759
800-503-9624
Woodlanders
1128 Colleton Ave.
Aiken, SC 28901
803-648-7522

Bulbs

Dutch Gardens
P.O. Box 200
Adelphia, NJ 07710
800-818-3861

McClure & Zimmerman
P.O. Box 368
Friesland, WI 53935
414-326-4220

Van Bourgondien
P.O. Box 1000
Babylon, NY 11702
800-622-9997

Roses

Antique Rose
Emporium
Rt. 5, Box 143
Brenham, TX 77833
409-836-9051

Jackson & Perkins
P.O. Box 1028
Medford, OR 97501
800-292-4769

Royall River Roses
70 New Gloucester Rd.
North Yarmouth, ME
04097
800-820-5830

Herbs

Mountain Valley
Growers
38325 Pepperweed Rd.
Squaw Valley, CA
93675
209-338-2775

Sandy Mush Herb
Nursery
316 Surrett Cove Rd.
Leicester, NC 28748
704-683-2014

Sunnybrook Farms
9448 Mayfield Rd.
P.O. Box 6
Chesterland, OH 44026
216-729-7232

Fruits

Northwoods Nursery
27635 S. Oglesby Rd.
Canby, OR 97013
503-266-5432

Raintree Nursery
391 Butts Rd.
Morton, WA 98356
360-496-6400

Stark Brothers
P.O. Box 10
Louisiana, MO 63353
800-325-4150

Tropicals

Brudy's Exotics
P.O. Box 820874
Houston, TX
77282-0874
800-926-7333
Web Site Catalog:
   http://www.brudys-exotics.com

Glasshouse Works
Church Street
Stewart, OH 45778
740-662-2142
Web Site Catalog:
   http://www.glass-houseworks.com

Logee's Greenhouses
141 North Street
Danielson, CT 06239
203-774-8038

Stokes Tropicals
P.O. Box 9868
New Iberia, LA
70562-9868
800-624-9706
Web Site Catalog:
   http://www.stokes-tropicals.com

Supplies

Gardener's Supply Co.
128 Intervale Road
Burlington, VT 05041
800-234-6630

Gardens Alive!
5100 Schenley Place
Lawrenceburg, IN
47025
812-537-8650

Peaceful Valley Farm
Supply
P.O. Box 2209
Grass Valley, CA 95945
916-272-4769

Worm's Way
3151 S. Highway 446
Bloomington, IN
47401
800-274-9676

Water Gardening Plants and Equipment

Lilypons Water Gardens
P.O. Box 10
Buckeystown, MD
21717
(also locations in Texas
   and California)
800-723-7667

Perry's Water Gardens
1831 Leatherman
Gap Rd.
Franklin, NC 28734
704-369-2056

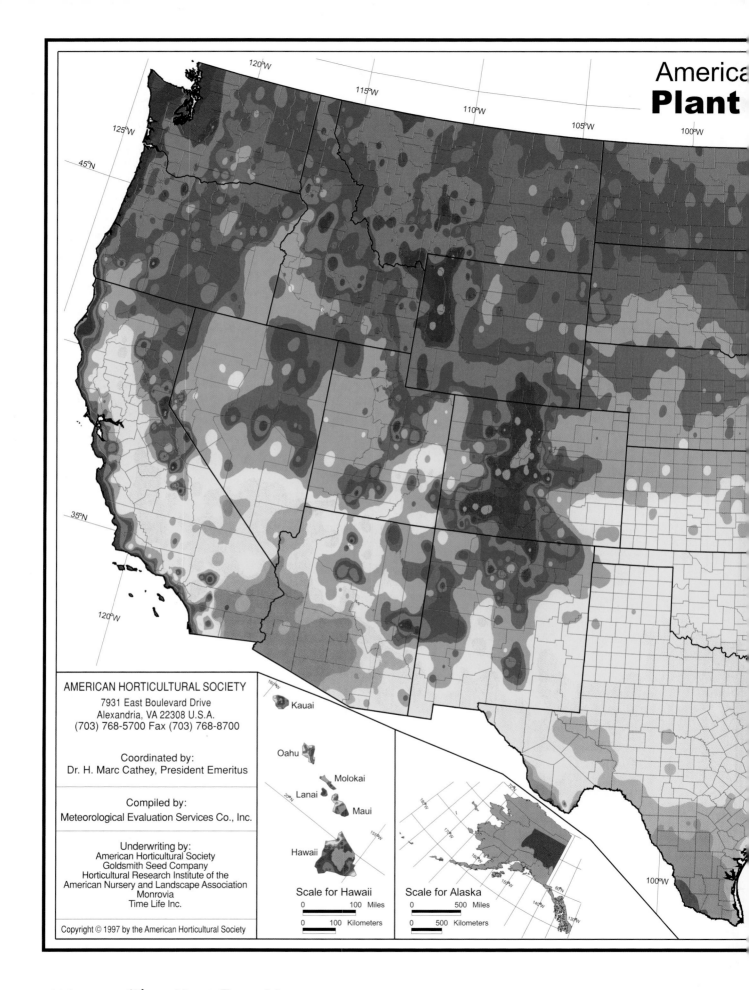

America
Plant

AMERICAN HORTICULTURAL SOCIETY

7931 East Boulevard Drive
Alexandria, VA 22308 U.S.A.
(703) 768-5700 Fax (703) 768-8700

Coordinated by:
Dr. H. Marc Cathey, President Emeritus

Compiled by:
Meteorological Evaluation Services Co., Inc.

Underwriting by:
American Horticultural Society
Goldsmith Seed Company
Horticultural Research Institute of the
American Nursery and Landscape Association
Monrovia
Time Life Inc.

Kauai

Oahu

Molokai
Lanai

Maui

Hawaii

Scale for Hawaii

0   100   Miles

0   100   Kilometers

Scale for Alaska

0   500   Miles

0   500   Kilometers

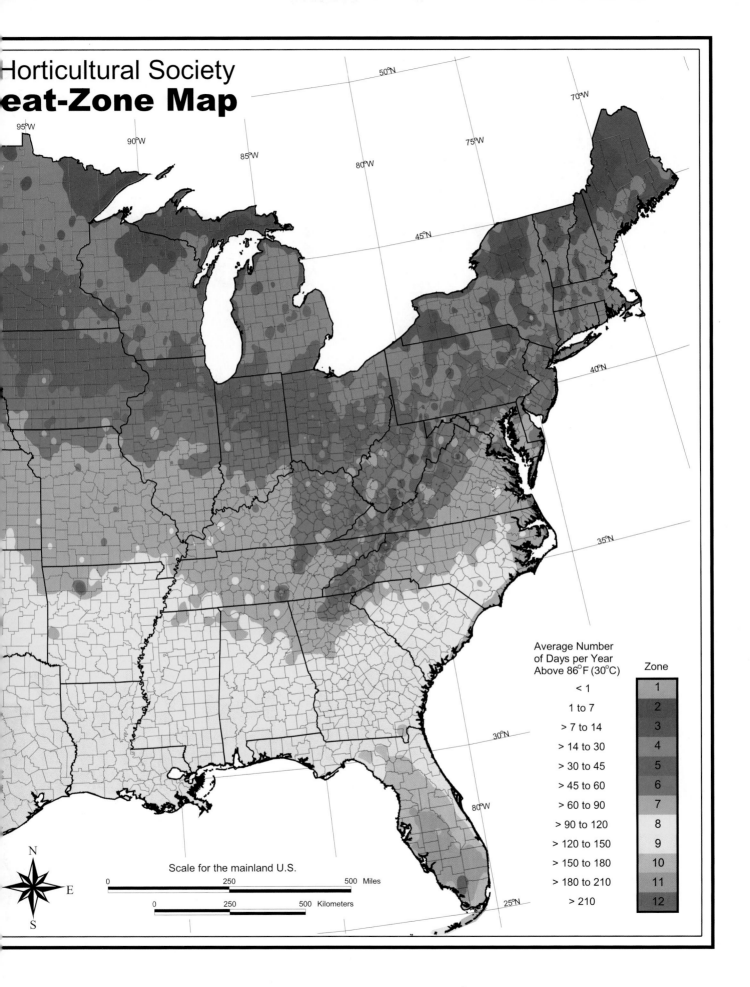

Average Number
of Days per Year
Above 86°F (30°C)   Zone

< 1	1
1 to 7	2
> 7 to 14	3
> 14 to 30	4
> 30 to 45	5
> 45 to 60	6
> 60 to 90	7
> 90 to 120	8
> 120 to 150	9
> 150 to 180	10
> 180 to 210	11
> 210	12

Scale for the mainland U.S.

0   250   500 Miles

0   250   500 Kilometers

N
E
S

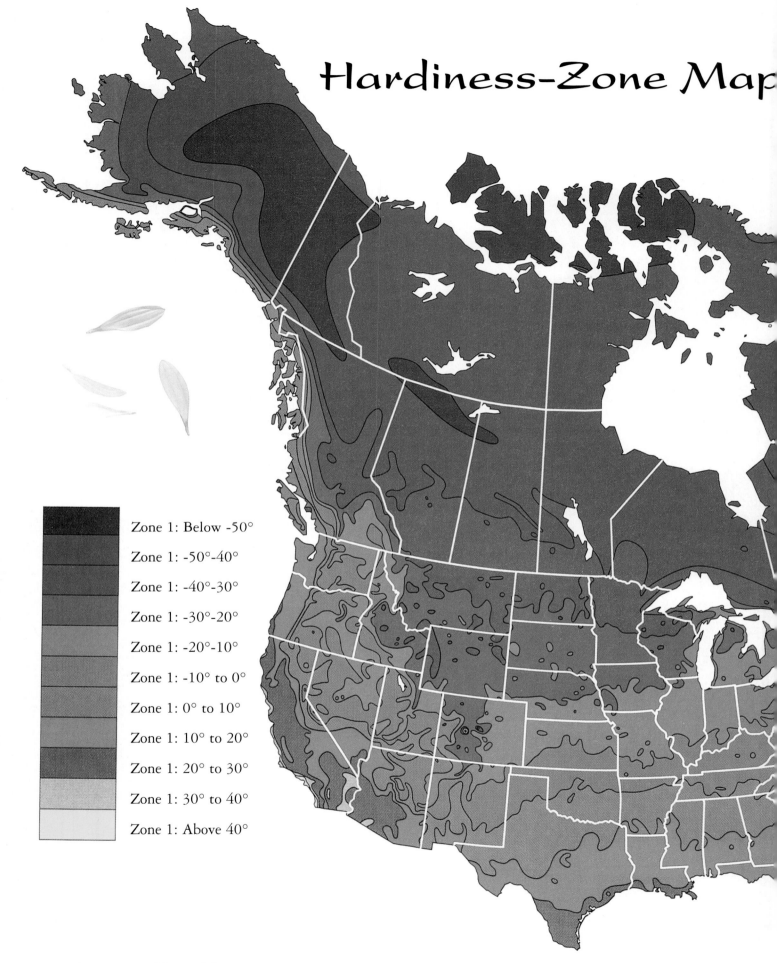

Hardiness-Zone Map

Zone 1: Below -50°
Zone 1: -50°-40°
Zone 1: -40°-30°
Zone 1: -30°-20°
Zone 1: -20°-10°
Zone 1: -10° to 0°
Zone 1: 0° to 10°
Zone 1: 10° to 20°
Zone 1: 20° to 30°
Zone 1: 30° to 40°
Zone 1: Above 40°

Average Dates of Last Spring Frost

	June
	May
	April
	March
	February
	January

Average Dates of First Fall Frost

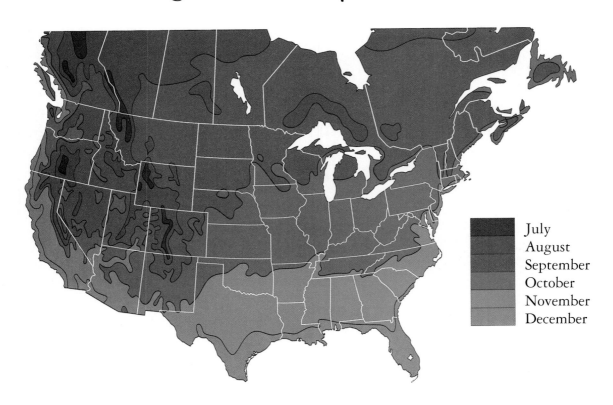

	July
	August
	September
	October
	November
	December

Index

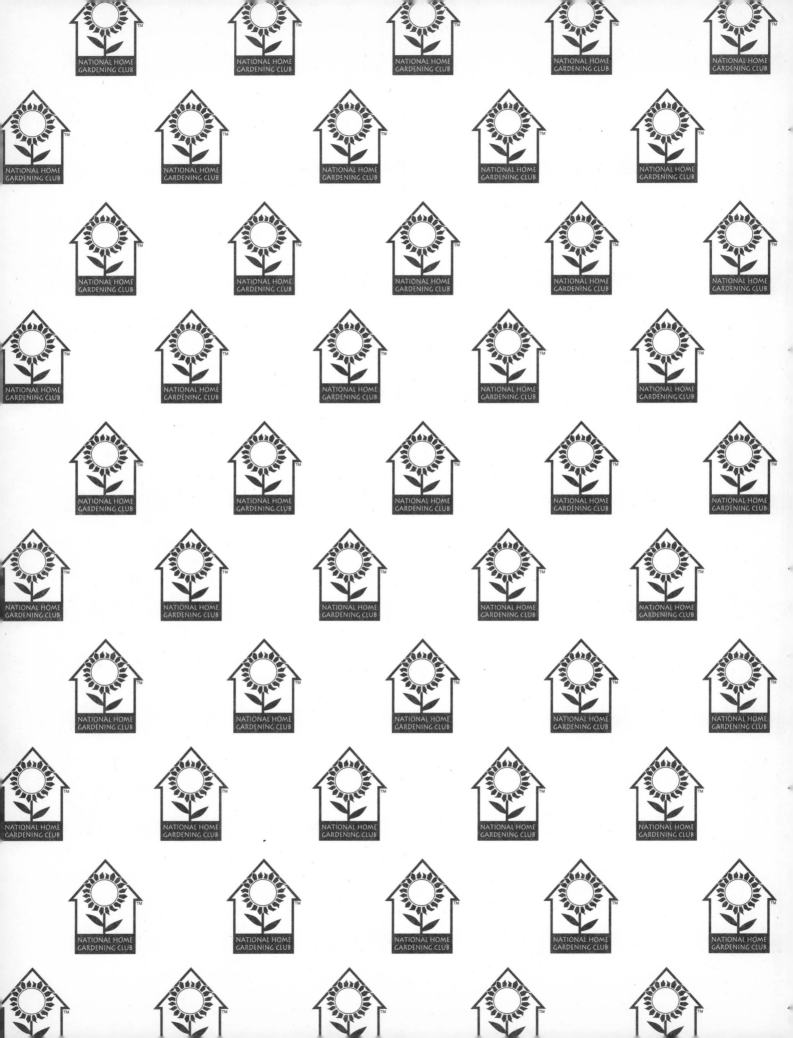